THE POINT

Where Teaching & Writing Intersect

THE POINT

Where Teaching & Writing Intersect

Edited by Nancy Larson Shapiro & Ron Padgett

Teachers&Writers
New York

This book is made possible by a grant from the
National Endowment for the Arts in Washington,
D.C., a federal agency.

Teachers & Writers also receives funding for
its publications from the New York State Council
on the Arts.

This year the Teachers & Writers publications
program is supported by a special grant from
The New York Community Trust.

Printed by Philmark Lithographics, New York, N.Y.

Teachers & Writers Collaborative
84 Fifth Avenue
New York, N.Y. 10011

Acknowledgements

In addition to funds from the New York State
Council on the Arts and the National Endowment
for the Arts, Teachers & Writers Collaborative's
work has been supported by the many schools in
the New York City area that have sponsored
residencies by writers and artists. T&W has been
able to survive and grow because of funding from
foundations, corporations, and other agencies
over the last 15 years. We sincerely thank the
following: American Airlines, American Broadcasting
Companies, American Stock Exchange, AT&T Long
Lines, Vincent Astor Foundation, Atari Institute
for Educational Action Research, Avon Products
Foundation, Bankers Trust Company, Chase Manhattan
Bank, CBS/Broadcast Group, Chemical Bank, Citibank,
Consolidated Edison, Equitable Life Assurance
Society, Exxon Education Foundation, Ford Foundation,
Edward W. Hazen Foundation, Heckscher Foundation for
Children, International Paper Company Foundation,
Kulchur Foundation, Mobil Foundation, Morgan
Guaranty Trust Company, National Broadcasting
Company, New York City Department of Cultural
Affairs/Arts Connection--Arts Exposure, New York
Community Trust, New York Council for the Humanities,
New York Foundation, New York Foundation for the
Arts, New York Times Company Foundation, Newsweek,
Henry Nias Foundation, Overseas Shipholding Group,
J.C. Penney Company, Ellis L. Phillips Foundation,
RCA, Helena Rubinstein Foundation, Scherman
Foundation, Surdna Foundation, and Variety Club
of New York. We also thank our many individual
contributors and members.

Contents

Preface

This collection of poems, short fiction, and
essays on teaching writing came out of a conversation that Ron Padgett and I began about a
year ago and that still continues. We have been
mulling over the sometimes subtle, sometimes
startling influences writers and their students
have on each other. We've also been trying to
pin down precisely what happens to the *writing*
(of writers *and* students) as a result of these
influences. Finally, we've been discussing
Teachers & Writers Collaborative--now over 15
years old--attempting to clarify what aspects
of the organization's approach to teaching writing
distinguish us and define the roles we play in the
literary and educational communities.

A group of writers and educators formed the
Collaborative originally as one remedy to the
dismal state of writing in the schools. Their
idea was to send writers into classrooms to get
kids involved in serious and playful imaginative
writing. They also wanted to show students--
who had no experience with or understanding of
contemporary literature--that "real" writers
write from their own personal experiences and
about things that matter to them. Too often,
children's writing had been preordained by the
expectations and limitations set by textbook
publishers. T&W writers set out to find and
nurture children's "authentic" voices.

What has come down to us from those early
years is a continuing concern for what the students
are trying to *say*--that is, for the *meaning*
struggling to come through even when the mechanics
need work. T&W writers still prod and coax their
students: *show us, really show, what you think,
feel, dream, in your own words, yes, but also in*

language you reach for, trying to get the precise word, the exact image, the unexpected idea. In short, the writers bring to their teaching the same concerns they have when they write.

The writers also teach motivational techniques they have found work for them. T&W's publications like *The Whole Word Catalogue 1* and *2* prove that these strategies can be passed along to others. But an outline of methods provides only the bare bones of what happens between teacher and students. Fortunately, many T&W writers have also kept diaries and done in-depth articles to give us a meatier view of their teaching. Not much has been written, however, on the connections between teaching and writing and the impact these links have on the writing itself. That's why we commissioned these essays.

The essays we present here take off in a number of directions. Some capture a special time when a writer and student came up against--and resolved-- similar artistic problems. Others, more general, focus on the surprising influence teaching has had on the style or subject matter of a writer's work. Together these essays and writings help us get closer to something we might call aesthetic pre- ference. This elusive element influences all aspects of the writers' work: what and how they write and what and how they teach. The literary models brought to class, the assignments given, the elements of language emphasized, the attitudes embodied in the writer, all these affect what students finally put down on paper. One of Kenneth Koch's students wrote, "I was born nowhere / And I live in a tree / I never leave my tree / It is very crowded / I am stacked up right against a bird" (see page 57). Would that stunning last line come out the same way with a different teacher? For each writer, of course, aesthetic preferences vary vastly and wonderfully. It is this intensely *personal* approach to teaching that is the hallmark of the Collaborative.

Although not all T&W writers are represented here--that would result in an enormous tome--we do have an excellent cross-section of writers who have built T&W over the years. Their essays reaffirm the original idea of the Collaborative: that the writers teach not just the *act* of writing but also the *art* of writing. That's the point of their 15 years of work.

--Nancy Larson Shapiro

Neil Baldwin

BRENDA SAYS

the Starlite Drive-In Theatre
hasn't been open for a year.
And now, mid-March, the sky
off-white from a fine rain

the Starlite Drive-In Theatre
stands movieless
among shopping plazas

Will we never get used
to broad parking lots
fringed with old snow?

I imagine a warm July
night. We're at
the Starlite Drive-In Theatre
watching something
go by
        on the screen

Brenda was the only person in room 208 of LaSalle
High School when I walked in that chilly morning
in March ten years ago to begin teaching the
first writing residency of my career. She was
standing with her back to me, gazing out the window through dusty slats of Venetian blinds. The
traffic hissed by along busy Niagara Falls Boule-
vard.

    "I like to come here early, before the other
kids," she explained, before I could say anything.
"I like to have time to settle my thoughts. And
we're going to write poetry, right? I figure it's
important to be calm and collected before we

start."

Nervous, unaccustomed to the company of people half my age, I stood next to her, shared her
view of the world at that moment. It wasn't too
lovely, but the rain helped soften the seemingly
endless, bleak succession of fast-food outlets,
steak houses, department stores with names like
K-Mart and Two Guys, gas stations, and more gas
stations.

"You see that place, Mr. Baldwin?" Brenda
pointed directly across the highway at a desolate,
abandoned lot, the blacktop blackened by rain.
"That was the Starlite Drive-In Theatre. Every
time I see it, I feel sad.... That was where my
boyfriend Jeff and I had our last date, before
we broke up last year, and it's been closed ever
since. When I see it, I can't help thinking of
him...."

"But you come in here every day and make sure
to look at it--so it can't bother you too much,
can it?"

She reflected for a moment. "Well, I feel
sad, but it's a nice kind of sad, you know? It's
kind of...kind of...."

"Nostalgic," I filled in, and sensing she
wanted me to explain but didn't want to ask me,
I went on, "a bittersweet, homesick feeling for
the past, longing for the good old days...."

The classroom door banged open, and the rest
of the students in second period English streamed
in, quickly, noisily. Despite ourselves, Brenda
and I exchanged disappointed looks. She took her
seat in the front row, folded her hands in front
of her on the desk, and waited.

I don't remember how that first class went.
But on the long drive back to my home in Buffalo,
I couldn't stop thinking about our tête-à-tête.

Here I was, with my newly-minted Ph D, fresh
from four years of graduate school, having written
a long, exhaustive dissertation on William Carlos

Williams. From those intensive years of study, I
had taken one overriding principle: the world
closest to hand, the *local,* was the inspiration
that fuelled the imagination to make poems. Upon
that conviction, Williams built a lifetime of
work, and a multifaceted epic, *Paterson.* It made
a lot of sense to me, theoretically.

But, no, I did not take that ideology into
the classroom with me. Instead, I had been de-
termined to rely upon traditional, formal lessons
in "form": sonnet, haiku, sestina. A novice
teacher, I was desperate for a set pattern.

In one brief conversation, a ninth-grader
changed all that. The change began with my own
poem, composed in a reverie-filled frame of mind
while driving. When I got to my apartment, I
dashed into the study, and the lines came, rat-a-
tat-tat.

When I teach, I value above all else, the
children's *familiarity* with family, friends,
neighborhoods, memories, and dreams. This is what
we write about, this is how we construct a curric-
ulum together, out of the materials of their im-
portant--never common--lives.

Barbara Baracks

(From a work-in-progress)

I was wondering at the rhythmic crashing sound
coming from the apartment above in the daytime.
Too huge for sex, too regular for an accident.
Tiny cracks formed in the ceiling's plaster. I'd
be taking a nap or watching "Ryan's Hope"--and
bam. It wasn't something you could get used to,
like a refrigerator hum, or something admirable,
like thunder. It was something that could drive
you nuts. And in those days, a year-and-a-half
ago, it didn't look like it'd take much.

I tried to visualize what I heard. Maybe it
was someone with an artifical leg made of lead,
dropped on the floor as he worked a slow and painful way to the refrigerator for a beer. Maybe it
was an invalid falling out of bed. Maybe someone
was trying to take apart the bathtub. These images didn't fit in with the unassuming family--
mother, father, three kids--I saw troop up and
down the stairs. They were a little frayed at the
edges, but then in this building that was doing
pretty good, most people here weren't so much
frayed as tattered. I know I was. I'd be sitting
at home with my tv, and there'd be this sledgehammer on my head.

Finally one day, after forty-five minutes of
this, I couldn't bear it. Shy as a new bride, I
went up the stairs and knocked on their door.
The mother opened up, a tired face, and behind her
two of her children, small ones. They were sitting on the floor, facing each other. As I stood
there, with great delight they struggled to their
feet, lifted between them--and dropped--a bowling
ball. Then they paused to stare at the stranger.
I wasn't that interesting.

They sat again. The smaller one, maybe five,
stood up alone now, strained, and raised the ball
a few inches by himself. I braced myself. It

crashed. The mother didn't flinch. Behind her,
the hallway stretched out to the living room.
The whole floor was covered with dents.

"Yes?" she said. I'd been silent for a number of seconds.

"It's about that," I said.

Her face didn't change.

"About the bowling ball," I continued. "Why
do you let them drop it?" My voice was as ordin-
ary as possible.

But it was as if I'd tossed a match into her
face. "Why shouldn't I?" Her fatigue instantly
rearranged itself into anger. "It keeps them
away from television. And what's it your business, anyway?"

Going back downstairs, I decided it was time
to get a job.

It looked like the Midwest with a nearby ocean.
On an endless plain dotted with occasional houses
and shacks the subway--here an elevated--ran a
lonesome straight line from horizon to horizon.
Half a mile's brisk walk down a cracked asphalt
street led me to the second-highest structure in
the landscape: a proper New York city three-
story brick elementary school. The highest struc-
ture--about a mile away--was a family of high-
rises, whose population of children trooped to
this school set in grand windy isolation.

Because I was as new to teaching as I was
to Far Rockaway, I walked to the school simmering
with stage fright. My best urbane manners got
me past the school guard, through the office, to
the handshake with the principal, and a tour down
the hallway to the door of the first class I ever
taught. Though, as I wrote in my notes that
evening, "the fear could have knocked me down,"

at least, standing at the brink of this sixth-
grade classroom, I had a plan.

A plan, I'd found, was not all that easy to
hatch. How convey in public the private act of
writing? Sweating it out the night before, I'd
fallen back on my writer's instinct (as well as
the spirit of a couple T&W meetings I'd already
attended) to approach teaching the same way I'd
approach writing: whatever is a live issue for
me will generate my liveliest presentation--
whether it's to a reading public or a roomful of
children.

In fiction and in journalism-as well as in my
person--I am unabashedly a nosy individual. I
tend to be proud of this the way some people are
proud of their discretion. I walk around in life
asking people how they know what they think they
know. And then I go to intricate lengths extrap-
olating from this a written fabric of my own
making.

A pristine form of this method is the riddle.
Looking at the thirty or so eleven-year-olds
looking back at me, I began. "Today, I woke up,
went into the kitchen, poured something into a
glass. This liquid was cold and bitter and went
down my throat like a spear. What was I drinking?"

It didn't take many guesses to hit on orange
juice. "But," a girl said. "It could have been
grapefruit juice instead."

"Or iced coffee," someone else said.

"You're right. My description isn't very
good. How could it be better, without making it
easy, giving it all away?"

The class elaborated many ways to describe
the act and feeling of drinking orange juice. I
wrote the result on the board: a long, metaphor-
laden, improbably detailed description of an
everyday experience. And the careful reader, after weighing and sifting all this observation,

would have to deduce orange juice.

We ran through one or two more out loud--
a brother snoring in bed, and so forth. And then
we switched to paper. "Remember," I coached,
"you're going to read these out loud, so make them
good and hard to guess."

While they wrote I allowed myself some exhilaration. Too bad, I thought, it's harder to get
myself to write than it is to get these kids
working. One piece of writing in this first
class, by Derrick Jordan, went beyond the riddle
form entirely, to pose, like all good prose, many
subtle questions:

"I heard weird noises downstairs in the living
room, falling boxes and sounds of dropping plates.
Then I heard deep, deep voices whispering. And
all of sudden loud screams in the other room. My
hands were trembling, my eyes stuck in, out, feel
paralyzed, can't move a muscle. Seeing bags being
thrown around man in blue suit. Beating, the
heavy voice men take him in a blue and white car.
And then it was over."

Jonathan Baumbach

FIRST NIGHT

I am urinating when my father, an angry look on
his face, comes into the bathroom. His standing
behind me--I can feel the heat of his impatience--
impedes me to a trickle. A watched urination can
be an infinite drag. "Save some for a rainy day,"
he says, jiggling the change in his pocket. I
leave unfinished, having to brush shoulders with
him to get to the sink. His face the color of
iodine, swollen and bruised. Why in God's name,
I think, didn't I lock the fucking door?

Washing my hands while he goes. I can't
distinguish the running faucet from the going
father. "It's all yours," I say. But then he is
also through and facing me. He puts his large
hand on my shoulder. "Why did you tell the po-
lice we wanted to kill you?" "I didn't," I say.
"It wasn't me." I can see from his eyes that he
doesn't believe me. "Go down and eat," he says
gruffly. "Mother is waiting."

On the black stairs going down, I remember
they are trying to poison me. My mother, slaving
over the stove, is wearing a nurse's mask to keep
her germs off the food. And yellow rubber gloves
because her hands, she says, are allergic to water. The combination strikes me as sinister.

"I'm not hungry," I tell her. "I'm going
out if you don't mind to stretch my legs."

"I made what you like," she whispers through
the mask, "your favorite. I gave you the last
of the Cuban bananas. You know how dear those
are. Dad will be beside himself when he finds
out."

At my place is a bowl of soggy Rice Krispies
with slices of rotten bananas on top. I hate
cold cereal, which she ought to know by now.

It's his favorite, *his*. When she's not looking
I scrape the stuff into the garbage, smacking my
lips to give the illusion of eating.

"Keep your mouth closed when you chew," she
says, pulling at her gloves. "Only pigs and pot-
ters eat with their mouths open."

We listen to my father coming down the steps.
He has a heavy walk. Fifty percent of his weight,
he once told me--a special family characteristic--
was in his feet.

"You're the only one in the family who's not
fussy about eating," she says in a voice loud
enough for the neighbors to hear. "If it weren't
for my little man, all my culinary gifts would be
as nothing."

My father is still clumping down the stairs.
What's taking him so long? "If he smells the
bananas on your breath," she says, "he'll have a
fit. You know how he loves those Cuban bananas."

I am thinking of hiding in the oven when for
no apparent reason she clamps a rubber-gloved hand
over my mouth. Her intentions are not clear to
me. I have the sense that the woman posing as my
mother is the murderer.

"If you don't tell him I gave you the bananas, I won't tell him that you ate them. Is it
a deal?"

I can hear him clumping down the stairs,
whistling a few bars of Stravinsky's *Petrouchka*--
the only music he knows.

Breaking away from my mother's rubber glove,
I run into my father at the bottom of the stairs.

"Wait for me in the car," he says in a tough
voice.

I go out into the car, my father a step behind. My mother in the kitchen screaming at the
top of her voice, "Don't Carl, don't, Carl,
don't."

Curious, I think getting into the powder blue
Oldsmobile (the upholstery made from old lamp
shades), my father's name isn't Carl. "I ate
the last of the bananas," I tell him.

9

"Just shut up, you," he says, crying. "No
one asked you. Did anyone ask you?"
     The car hits someone backing out, a boy with
glasses on a bicycle, a former friend.

(From *ReRuns,* The Fiction Collective, New York,
N.Y., 1974)

WRITING TEACHING

I am writing this piece about teaching writing in
order to find out why I do what I do. The act
of writing is a step into consciousness.
     In the past few years, I've been working
mostly with advanced writing students, many of
whom have developed a high level of skill before
coming to my class. I teach in the fiction component of the MFA Program in Creative Writing at
Brooklyn College. The students are all ages, are
interesting, talented, limited, blocked, prolific,
represent a range (sometimes it seems the whole
spectrum) of styles and visions. They have their
commitments, their ways of seeing (and not seeing)
and I have mine. My job, as I see it, is to enter a student's fictional world no matter its
distance from my own and deal with that world on
its own best terms. I try to help my students
clarify their impulses, help them be more articu-
lately and surprisingly themselves. That may be
the only conscious intention I allow myself.
     The gratifications in working with advanced
students are less obvious than those of working
with beginners. The beginner has the possibility
of making astonishing progress, of going from
nowhere to somewhere, from nothing to something.
The more skill writers have, the more locked in
they tend to be to what they already do well--

the province of their authority. Skill without
an overriding vision can be self-limiting. At
times I prod students to take risks, to do things
they feel uncomfortable doing. It is no secret
that we learn most from our failures. A writer
(like anyone, like everyone) either advances or
loses ground, moves ahead or falls into self-imi-
tation. With both beginning students and the more
advanced, I want to push writers toward eccentri-
city, toward their most distinctive and surprising
impulses.

     The only constant in my method as a teacher
is to keep changing what I do, a way of keeping
myself from getting stale. It pleases me to believe that I teach the way I write, making things
up as I go along, though who knows? I have no
theories of how to teach writing, have kept my
distance from awareness of methodology. I have
few conscious techniques, and I tend to discard
them as they make themselves known to me. I
have little sense of what I am going to say to
students about their work before I say it. I like
to engender a condition of risk and trust to instinct, or hope for revelation, to get me through.
This method (or non-method) works for me more
often than not. I often discover what I think
about a student's work, engage perhaps my deepest
feelings about it, in the process of articulating
what I didn't know I knew.

     In the MFA I teach tutorials--one on one--
and workshops with a group of approximately ten.
My method in tutorial tends to be different with
each student. In the workshop, I read a student's
fiction out loud to the group, a story or part of
a novel all of us have already read to ourselves.
Each member of the group comments on the piece
while the writer listens in, sometimes takes
notes, restrains the urge to justify the writing.
I usually save my remarks for last, though I strive
to avoid predictability. Even after everyone has
had a say, the author has the freedom to explain

or to refuse to explain himself/herself. The point is to let the writing speak for itself and for the author to get a chance to reexperience the story as if it were written by someone else. (I realize that this sounds like method, but it is not something I articulated to myself before writing this essay.) The workshop tends to be useful to writers no matter, sometimes it appears, what I do. Writers get both criticism and support, a sense of audience, a sense of others in similar struggle. Student pieces influence one another, suggest other ways of approaching story. A community of mutual interest and trust gradually emerges.

In order to generate an occasion for this essay, I gave my workshop a writing assignment; read them the opening chapter of my novel, *Reruns,* a work composed of what I think of as transformed dreams; and asked my students to write a dream (or short dreamlike narrative) of their own. It is not something I had done with this group before. The virtue of any assignment is that it enforces focus. It is also, paradoxically, liberating in that it frees writers from the responsibility they feel toward their own choices of subject or mode. Also, writing a dream, in which theoretically anything can happen, frees the writer from the demands of credibility and verisimilitude. In a dream story, the writer has license to be incredible. Still, it is not necessarily easier to write a dream than to imitate waking reality.

The most obvious way to write a dream is by transcribing an actual one before it slips away into ether. But dreams, like remarks, are not in themselves literature. The writer must give the dream the rudiments of form, must carry its odd narrative through to the implications of its illogical logic. The invented dream, if it is right, comes from the same source (the dazzling code language of the unconscious) as an actual dream.

The assignment produced surprising results, particularly from writers who had been working in realistic modes. One piece seemed to me more resonant and powerful than anything the writer had done before. The writer, a woman, had been writing a novel about a failed marriage and had had difficulty imagining material that had not taken place in her "real" life. In the dream the same obsessive material was brought to life in a way it had never been in the writer's realistic novel. It will be interesting to see whether the impact of the dream, its resonance and clarity, will carry over into revisions of the novel. In any event, I'll probably use the assignment again, or an assignment like it, or an altogether different assignment.

Judith Binder

From THE CHICKEN MADE OF RAGS, a children's play

(The following excerpt begins with the Chicken
Made of Rags receiving an invitation to the Banquet at the Big Hotel. She starts out and picks
up lots of friends along the way. This short
selection starts toward the end of the walk.)

Exterior. Glass Palace Greenhouse in Golden Gate
Park.

*Bees are swarming around a flower. The Swan is
shooing them away with her white lace hankie. She
smells the flower. Her white-gloved hand is holding the white-gloved hand of her tiny daughter.
They are dressed alike and both hold white lace
purses. They both bring their lacy white hand-
kerchiefs up to their mouths to cover delicate
coughs. They are in the midst of a lush garden
where a gardener is putting in a new plant; the
mother Swan directs his activity.*

SWAN, *pointing to the left:* It would be a little
more charming if the tulips were closer to the
daffodils, don't you think?

*The Gardener starts to dig a hole for the tulips.
Little Swan sees the Chicken, Duck, and Rooster.*

LITTLE SWAN: Look who's coming!!!

SWAN, *waving them over:* Ah, dear friends...(*She
coughs into her hankie; Little Swan does too.*)
Lovely day. (*She turns back to the Gardener,
directing his activity further.*) Now a little
to the right where the precious petals can catch
the late morning sun. (*Turning back to the other
three as the Gardener grunts and carries out her
orders.*) Where are you going, Chicken Made Of

Rags and Duck and Rooster?

CHICKEN: Oh, we're going to a banquet at the Big Hotel.

DUCK: A *grand* banquet!

ROOSTER: Harumph...I'm just going along for the walk in case anything needs fixing.

Swan coughs; Little Swan coughs too.

SWAN: How I wish that I could go. *(She looks back to the Gardener.)* Now a bit to the left. We wouldn't want the little petals scorched. *(Turning to her guests.)* They must have sent me an invitation too, but lost my address and are searching everywhere to find it. Perhaps I should save them the trouble and simply come along with you. *(She ties a bonnet on Little Swan.)*

LITTLE SWAN: We'll come along!

CHICKEN: Hurry then. We don't want to be late.

Swan puts a lace shawl over Little Swan's shoulders and they join the others. The Chicken, Duck, Rooster, Big Swan, and Little Swan flutter, waddle, strut, and glide off. The Gardener whistles the walk music happily and carries on his work.

Exterior. Chinatown.

The walk music is heard. The walkers pass a vegetable stand. The store window is full of signs in Chinese. The vegetable man is watering his vegetables. He waves. They cut through a playground where the Chinatown elders are playing checkers. They nod and wave to the passing party.

*They turn a corner, cross the street and walk
along the pier. The walk music is interrupted
by the sound of a stone hitting the water.*

Exterior. Fishing Pier.

*The sound is the sinker on the Goose's fishing
line, which has just been cast. Ripples and cir-
cles and waves form around it. The Goose sees the
reflections of the Chicken, Duck, Rooster, and
Swans in the water, and looks up as they approach.
She is wearing overalls and a brightly colored
kerchief.*

GOOSE, *whispering loudly:* Hi, Chicken Made Of
Rags, Duck, Rooster, Swan, and Little Swan.

CHICKEN, DUCK, ROOSTER, *and* SWANS, *in unison:*
Hello, Goose!

GOOSE, *whispering:* Shhh! Speak softly. The fish
will be scared away.

The others nod that they understand.

Where are you all going?

CHICKEN, *whispering:* We're going to a banquet at
the Big Hotel.

DUCK, *whispering:* Wow!

ROOSTER, *whispering:* I, of course, am just walking
along in case anything needs fixing.

SWAN, *whispering:* My invitation was probably lost
along the way, so I'm just going along to save the
hotel the trouble of sending another invitation.

LITTLE SWAN, *in a loud voice:* Me too!!!

GOOSE, *whispering:* Shhh! *(Pointing to her line.)* You'll frighten the fish. When is this banquet?

CHICKEN, *whispering:* Tonight at six o'clock.

GOOSE, *in a normal voice:* Well . . .it's getting a little noisy here for fishing. *(She reels in her line and packs up.)* I might as well come a-long with you.

CHICKEN: Yes. But hurry along. We don't want to be late!

(From *Scripts* magazine)

Based on an old Cuban folk tale, *The Chicken Made Of Rags* is a script I wrote in collaboration with Nina Serrano in 1972. It is impossible to separate the script into Nina's words and my words; it is as if it had been written by one person. Other collaborators and I wrote scripts in which scenes were written separately, then put together. In *The Chicken Made Of Rags,* however, every word was written while both writers were present, and lines started by one person were often finished by the other.

The many scripts I have written in collaboration were some of the most artistically and personally satisfying writing experiences I've had. Nina and I didn't know the now-popular term when we first started "collaborating." We called it the "Yes, and..." approach. Our three successful plays convinced us that our method works, and it's one I've used in my own writing, with or without others, and have passed along to my students.

I usually give students the option of writing
alone or collaborating in pairs on any play or
story they want to write, and tell them that the
first step is to write down anything either of
them says, even if it seems completely off the
track. "Don't argue," I caution, "always say yes.
Whatever doesn't belong will be discarded later."

Writing every thought down for the first
rough draft is easy. Yet, students have a hard
time with it at the beginning. They are as used
to disagreeing with each other as they are prone
to negate their own creative process. Indeed,
sometimes they are not wrong when they find their
partner's ideas bad. My own firm belief in the
process comes in handy at this point. I urge them
to plow ahead, write it down, and don't waste time
disagreeing. Keep up the momentum.

After Nina and I finished our first draft, we
broke it into small sections on separate cards,
each with a simple descriptive title to remind us
of what the section was about. It's so much
easier to move cards around than to search through
a written manuscript. This card game part of the
process gave us a start on editing out extraneous
sections. The editing and cutting process was
furthered during the reshuffling of the actual
script. Again the "Yes, and..." method works.
Getting rid of words is an important part of the
writing process. If either person felt it was
important to cut a word, it went out. Later we
might put some words back, but at this point it
seemed just as important to cut as it had been to
add at the beginning.

By collaborating, students get used to saying
yes to others, they find it easier to say yes to
themselves, and creative momentum builds. One
problem I anticipated was that one of the collabo-
raters might dominate and the other withdraw. I
decided to risk this, since my experience with

three different collaborators showed me that both
pull their own weight as long as they say yes. My
experience with students proved that the risk was
worth taking. Often one did dominate at first,
but the other soon picked up some skills from the
dominant one, and since everyone was instructed
never to say no (which is not to say they didn't
try), both writers contributed fully to the
work. It takes time and patience for teacher and
students, but the process proves successful, and
gives students skills not only for writing but
also for any area of their school lives in which
they have to work with others.

Carole Bovoso

ON THE "TALGO"

                    For Angel

You and I were on the train to Paris.
In the morning the lady in my compartment asked,
Is that your husband? And she was nodding yes
with her head,
signalling yes with her eyes, speaking to me on
other levels,
yes, say yes.
And I said yes.
Because we were as close as that, because we were
closer
than that because you were
more that than anything I could explain.
And I said yes, because that was the answer she
wanted
because of what she had to tell me,
and I said yes, because of all the answers, it was
most correct.
And I shouldn't have worried, because. . .
"Once I had a husband. . ."
she began. . .
Her Spanish clear, distinct.
Now she makes this journey each year, for
25 years.
The anniversary of a death.

SPECIAL MOMENTS

I have come to value certain special moments that
occur during my teaching residencies. At these
times there is a link between my students and me--
a direct communication between us. I have a
sense that there are things that we understand
that the outside world does not. It is these moments that make me feel special as a writer, feel
that my own work and life is fed, inspired, that
I have been fortunate enough to be able to open
myself up enough so that the children have been
able to *see* me and to *hear* my voice.

Oddly enough such moments are likely to happen not when I am discussing or reading my own
work, but rather when I am involved with explo-
ration of the work of some other writer, be it
that of a professional or one of the children.

This year I have had a rather high incidence
of such inspiring moments. Asked to work with my
classes on Writing from Direct Observation, I began to teach my kids the same kind of material I
develop for my adult Journal and Notebook Workshops. That is to say, precisely the same kind
of material that I develop for my own growth as
a writer and a woman.

Working in journals and notebooks (quite different from the daily logs many teachers prescribe)
involves being open to constant self-discovery.
Most children are not used to considering the or-
dinary events of their lives as subjects for
writing. They think that something must be
"special" in order to warrant attention. In answer to a question about what happened to them
this very morning before they left the house for
school, I often get "Nothing."

It is interesting, then, to unravel all the
details of what actually did happen and what might
have been important about it. The children soon

enjoy both noticing and writing about such things as a new red toothbrush and the way the toothpaste looked on its bristles, or the way the eggs turned out (the first two yolks broke, the third turned out perfect).

So the children and I have focused on observing many things: among them, things we never noticed before in the classroom, overheard conversations, all the things that happen in two minutes of "real" time. The observation is internal as well: we have noticed how emotions change from moment to moment and observed the elusive processes of dreams and memory. My work with dreams has been ongoing, and I have found them to be an endless source of fascination to both adults and children. We talk about what kinds of things happen in dreams and the different ways in which they can happen (when we seem to have super-powers, for example). Having discovered that people who fly in dreams have very particular methods for getting airborne, I have begun to collect flying methods: two hops and a jump and you're off, or spin around and around until you rise up, or lots of arm flapping, for example. One boy rather alarmingly had to be hit by a bus in his dreams before he could take off, unharmed, into the air.

Dreams are, of course, a timeless source of inspiration as well, and it is with a special kind of ease that children write about them and create work that is based on dream imagery and dream events, e.g., transformation of time and space, of landscape, of humans into other life forms or vice-versa.

> Dreaming I am
> inside the places I am
> Always knowing more
> than after or before.

During my first poetry residency in 1978 I developed this little poem, summing up my feeling about dreams, and I have always encouraged all my students to tap dream knowledge on a regular basis. Recently I sang a completely wordless song of my own devising, destined to create a state of mind akin to dreaming, during which the children could let images freely enter their minds. I had been inspired by Native American chants and the poet and musician Charlie Morrow's dream chants.

I then asked the class to tell me what images they saw during the dream chant, and there was a great deal of excitement as they spoke. We recorded the results and tried it again. Here is an example from a combined 3rd, 4th, 5th grade class:

GROUP DREAM POEM

A pink crystal is flying
A lot of Indians are sitting around a fire. There is a white horse standing behind them
A king crab is scuttling across the sand
A plane is crashing with green fire
A black horse with a white star on its forehead is standing next to a white horse with a black star on its forehead and there's a rabbit hopping next to it
A pink flower is blooming in a red cup with a million designs on it.

There was an excitement in the room about what seemed a new way of seeing, creating, and communicating with each other. By being shown how these images "popped" into their heads, the children were ready to pay attention to images that come at other times, images that are the poet's fuel.

My own work in prose and poetry continues to be fed by dreams and by the great wealth of

of material that finds its way into my journals.
And it continues to be inspired by the sometimes
elusive ways in which my students and I interact.
Compare this student poem with the preceding one
of my own.

A SPECIAL PLACE

One day in the Catskills I was
hiking and a bird whistled to
me and I whistled back and it whistled back to me
and again
and again and again we whistled
for hours and hours and hours.

                    --Mikel Washington, 3rd grade

Anne Cherner

THE REAPPRAISAL

The fledgling quivers in your hand,
its feathers still sticky from the albumen.
You want to think, "Poor blind thing,"
your own heart beginning to palpitate
at such a spectre of helplessness.
But you steel yourself;
you are stern and the world
is so full of suffering anyhow.

You could paper any attitude
with a justification.
The linoleum on the floor is warped
from too many scrubbings
and the same sad ballad
bleats from the black radio--
the bird, just-born, can't sing,
can't see, can barely
beat its blood back through
its terrified body.

Even if you spoke the same language,
what would you tell it?
That life, the accident,
is lucky after all,
that summer evenings, like the clamor
of myriad fluttering wings,
will call this being
to its moist green breast--
it's a lesson easy enough to minister
in a sombre time.

But you? Your lookout?
You're the one
the bird will leave here.
Take that into consideration.
You of the sleepless nights.

Was it the longing
for melodies you cannot memorize
that cupped your hands for acceptance?

Admit you desire
what you cannot have.
Shudder as you will, put it
from you, the cracked bits
of shell still litter
the floor at your feet.
It's a long way for a little one
to fall. *Don't let it happen.*

REGARDING "THE REAPPRAISAL"

Small but intense sensations--the swish of a pencil across paper and the faint cloud of a smudge
superimposed over neat, slanting script because
the pencil is being moved by a downcurved left
hand. An eraser also fades the blue lines ruled
on the paper, and the washed-out red of the left-
hand margin is always more prominent than the
right.
        I begin with the writing materials of every
schoolchild because teaching gave them to me
again, although, like everything adult, my
current versions are more refined: perfectly
round maroon draughting pencils that don't
callous the fingers, their butter-soft leads
sharpened to pin-sized points by a manual
sharpener of a solid and weighty brass that, unlike the mechanical sharpeners that Nabokov's
Pnin thought said "Ti-con-der-oga, ti-con-der-
oga," don't greedily devour half the pencil in
half a minute.
        When I am writing with these materials in the

stillness of my living room, I am not thinking
about teaching, but I suspect that the spectre
of a little girl also inhabits the quiet, medi-
tative atmosphere, for whom writing was also a
diversion, albeit a less disciplined one. I
sharpen my pencil, tap the sharpener against the
carved wooden ashtray I use for the shavings and
inhale the cool cellar odors of graphite and wood.

Sometimes I wonder what this ghost child would
make of one of my writing assignments, but she is
not in the classroom when I rivet the other pairs
of eyes on me, and then on the blackboard. The
children I have worked with in a fashionable corner
of Manhattan, in the ghettoes of Harlem and the
Bronx, suburban Westchester and Long Island, and
a Brooklyn as far removed as twenty years do not
bring me back to the Alabama schoolgirl of the
early sixties. And yet they have given me something else.

Reality on reality. The children do not necessarily see what I see. We are taught that
the planet rotates in the void, but what are the
ways by which we begin to accept it? And, if
we comprehended in advance where the truth would
bring us, would we want it? Children cannot
know the desperation of their childhood, that
its smallness is false, that it will change.
That is what adults know and desire to protect,
because it is what they once were themselves,
and now are not.

Under as much duress as I ever wrote any
poem, standing on a street corner in a frigid
January afternoon after teaching, my fingers numb,
I began to scribble the first lines that would become "The Reappraisal" and continued upon waking
the next morning at four a.m., anxious and appre-
hensive about the two-hour commute, also to teach,
that faced me in three hours. The poem is about
a love sparked by the helplessness of that object,
and it is what children have taught me while I

have taught them that with the right words they can describe what they formerly thought was inexpressible.

Jack Collom

●

nobility is the secret of my character,
my slight paunch a flowering of gentleness.
my poached-egg eyes contain the seed of wisdom.
my tantrums are keenly-perceived emotional ara-
    besques.
my compromises are selflessness making love to the
    world
my rotten teeth the restraint of brutality.
my shaking hands are joie de vivre.
my meaness is pure light.
my obscurity tantalizes everyone.
my blackouts are part of the music of time.
my cowardice is a beautiful dance.
my blandness is the space approaching God.
my murders are mutations of the unicorn.
my poems are bits of ice on the warm plains.

Dear Nancy & Ron--

    Re our recent conversation, here are my
feelings on the "me" side of the reciprocity between poet & student in school workshop activity.
    For one thing, teaching makes me rehearse my
thought and refine its presentation over and over,
without recourse to the jargon of literary criti-
cism--which can bestow a false aura of keen in-
tellection on a small pedestrian thought. In
class I have to say what I think about poetry in
brass-tacksy, simple American. This helps keep
me from spiralling off into some mental ivory
tower, keeps me in touch with my original feelings
about poetry.

Contact with children is like Antaeus bouncing off the earth, strengthens me in poetic feeling, since, as they say, the poet is sort of an over-grown, slightly disguised child (who has maybe learned how to cross the street) (and fill out forms).

The work, though intense, is a godsend, pro-fessionally, since you can work a little less than full-time and still buy baby a new shoe or two.

But, above all, it's good because it contin-uously excites me about poetry. The kids are not likely to be good at anything of versificatory intricacy or linguistic sophistication or "high" cultural reference. What we are left with-- what they *are,* again and again, good at--is a *freshness* with language--a vague, and oft-used word. But let me try to explain. In being immersed in children's poems, my focus is inevitably directed to the minute moves, the basic energies, of rhythm and word-choice and image--uncluttered by any pre-tension except the most transparent--in what we might call primitive written speech. I'll illus-trate with a few examples of what I call "lunes"-- a flexible haiku-derivative for which not syllables but words are counted--eleven words arranged 3/5/3. Here is a lune writ by a 5th grader, years ago:

> When the sun's
> rays hit the shades, it
> lights up lines.

(I had asked the class to look around them, if baffled for subject matter, and he saw the light striking through the Venetian blinds). This poem is extraordinarily physical. In the first place it recounts *only* the fact (and my proclivity in any case is to try to release the "primitive" energies in language and the senses--"no ideas but in things," a maxim I continue to admire).

Also, it's loaded with word-music: n and n forming
a swing in line 1, that simple rhythm repeated in
line 3 with the hot, different rhythm of line 2
tucked between, assonance of rays and shades,
rhyme of hit and it, repeated soft "the" sound,
repeated "uh" sound plus n and t in line 3, "li"
rhyme, way the vowels rise and fall -- all of
course non-calculated, just a good ear, a good
minute. And then, of course, the poem has im-
plications--*his* lines were lit up, in the piece
he wrote and beyond. Mental play opened up via
the word "shades," especially in conjunction with
basic sunlight.

Here are a few more lunes (from high school
students) that may best demonstrate that vivifying pure
energy of the best of children's poetry:

> if the rain
> was not wet it would
> probably be dry.

(I say damn the subjunctive, full speed ahead.
These are all best, I think, when the line-break
is emphasized by a breath-stop.)

> extra, extra, read
> all about it! there is
> no news today.

(Haiku-like last-line twist of wit, confounding
expectations.)

> a raindrop falls.
> it falls on my nose--
> delicate, light, transparent.

(Again a surprise, of rhythm and tone, in the
final line.)

31

well I did
but I wish I never
left my home.

when ducks fly
from the very still water
it becomes violent.

she reached up
and caught the little piece
of white fur.

you write with
a pencil tip bending lines
into your thoughts.

brains work hard:
the sound from gears grinding
drowns out thought.

load the ship.
go out to the sea.
don't come back.

No need, I think, to point out specifically
the ways in which these poems delight (and in-
struct). The only drawback is that the adult
poet may, abashed by such glee, feel inadequate
to transcend stodginess in his own work. Not
really. So its altogether like learning aero-
nautics from the birds, which I gather the en-
gineers continue to do. In sum, I find it inspiring to work with children in poetry workshops.
It allows me to exercise my human energy in just
the field I prefer. And it provides me with a
stream of what I regard as primal poetic example.

Yours sincerely,

Jack

Barbara Danish

JOURNAL EXCERPTS, JUNE 1982
Written in response to a teacher's request to
write continuously and explore the language incidents that went into making us the thinkers/
learners/writers we are.

(I notice myself taking time to prepare. I've
noticed this lately about myself--I used to not
want to do "research," that is, gather the in-
formation, figure out the task. Now I can't
seem to start right in. I can still do freewriting of course, but when there's an *assignment,* I
have to think. This is a nice feeling. I think
I used to be scared; I just needed to get anything down; I was in a rush to finish. Now I'm
more efficient--in a good way. Oh well, enough
of this. Does this happen when I'm aware of
audience? When I have an assignment? Will I
use this writing for myself? Can I transfer my
honesty from my journal to in-class writing?)
     I want to make a list of the formal and in-
formal learning and the part conversation played
in my life. Any mode, the teacher said. Okay
then--a list. I want to see what comes up.
     --I was reading *Exodus.* Blue book cover.
This must have been during elementary school?
5th-6th grade? D. said it was a hard book. Did
I understand it? I said yes. He wanted to be
sure so I was to tell him about what I had read.
What I remember is that I got to a part with sex--
and of course I couldn't talk to him about that--
so I stopped talking to him. Maybe I stopped
reading? What did I learn?
     (I just reread what I wrote. Is it okay to
reflect? Take time to think? It feels wrong.
Is it okay?)

--In fourth grade I wrote poems about dino-
saurs, and Miss Moore (pink walls) read my poem
to the class. She said she was giving me a poetic
license, and those she *never* gave out. In front
of the class. I think I learned I could get
praise this way. Rewarded. For some reason I was
proud of this poetic license. Why? Would anything she gave me in front of the class have been
valuable? Or did I have a notion of what this
was?

Sometimes I wonder if I've ever affected a
child's life the way Miss Moore affected mine.
(I keep wondering, am I doing this right? She
said it could be *any* topic--but I still want to
know--is it right?)

--Let's think about the conversations over
and over about trying things. (I really feel
like I'm going to cry. Really, if no one was
in this classroom right now I'd cry, I feel so
sad.)

"If you can't do it right, don't do it at
all."

"If you can't do it right the first time,
don't do it at all."

Why didn't I ever fight back?

Language is how I have my parents in my mind.
They live there--their words and their looks, and
I say their words to myself. It's time for you
to leave, Mom and Dad. I love you very much,
but it's time for you to leave.

--Memories about learning what kind of learner
I was.

I can't think. I have too much feeling
right now.

--Conversations/Experiences:

Me around age 10-11 to someone, someone I
felt very close to and was willing to confide in:
"I believe that if I could find Jesus' grave and
dig him up and give him food and water, he'd
live again. He died of hunger and thirst, didn't

he?" No response that I can remember. I didn't
offer those things very often.

    7th grade. 8th grade. 9th grade.

    --Oh yes! 6th grade? A wonderful day--I
had a peanut butter and bacon sandwich--what a
treat! Mrs. S gave us a math test on a very
light rexo. She went over the problems and told
us to pencil them in. I didn't. *I* could read
it! But I guess I couldn't. I got a lot wrong.
Is that possible? And in front of the whole class
she said, "Barbara thought she was so smart, and
now look at what happened to her." She moved my
desk away from everyone. I had to eat my sand-
wich alone. It tasted terrible. It stuck in my
throat. Okay, Mrs. S, I learned I wasn't smart.
Thank you for helping me learn that. I learned
the consequences of not doing what the authority
tells you to do. I was embarrassed. That was
vicious, Mrs. S, but I learned that your way was
the "right" way.

    This is a story of how I came to be the
learner/thinker/writer I am--not so much through
conversation as through commands (not the right
word) not through one incident, but through an
accumulation of incidents.

THE JOURNAL AS TEACHER

My journal was my first writing teacher. When I
teach, I imitate the way my journal taught me.

    What do I mean by this? How can a blank
book be a teacher? How do I imitate my journal?

    On August 4, 1964, I started my journal. I
was 15 years old and that, in part, accounts for
the entry:

    'Allo. 'Ow are y'ole chap? Quite nice to

meet you, I must say! J'ecrirai quelquechose en
francaise et quelquechose en Anglais. La francais
mienne n'a pas tres raison.

I dropped the "French" a week later but continued writing, until today, 18 years later, I
have over 50 volumes of my journal. I wouldn't
call these volumes a chronicle of my life--there
are too few events mentioned and too few details
of these events. Instead, I would say that for
me, these journals are like the lizard, that an-
imal from prehistoric times who still lives among
us, who reminds me of a time when the world was
roamed by creatures who did not have names for
things, and who did not know what was happening
to them, or why. I never intended for my journals to describe my life. I used them for whatever I needed at the time, and those needs suggest who I was.
When I was younger I am sure I kept one of
those fake red leather diaries. They had a few
lines for each day and a key that always got lost;
imagine, locked out from yourself! Those diaries
seemed to be for girls only and seemed to suggest
that a particular type of secret had to be told
in them. My first journal was a plain black and
white speckled composition book full of lined
pages. The keeping of the journal was my idea,
and the only rules were the ones I imposed on
myself. When I go back to my journals I notice
that one rule I kept for a long time, one that
prevails among inexperienced writers, was that of
disguise. Although I am sure that at the time I
believed I was writing honestly, now I see that I
was constantly disguising myself. I used foreign
languages ("Allo..."); I wrote about myself as
though I were in a teen novel ("We had lobster for
dinner--scrumsh!"); I had a qualification for
everything, subordinating all feelings to manners.
("It was *rather* good," *"quite* boring," "Hope it

all goes well"; that last one was a wish for two
classmates who had decided to fall in love with
each other even though I was in love with one of
them.) I wrote poetry, another disguise, since the
subject of the poems is always missing and the
poetry itself is undecipherable. My dreams were the
one way I consistently escaped the disguises, although they too are disguises of a sort.

I can understand my inclination to disguise.
Writing is dangerous. It is easy to write clichés
("I wanted to kill him") and generalizations ("Oh
sure I felt good about it")--those conventional
disguises that are so acceptable to others. It is
our own personal truth that is painful and dangerous to tell (and, I think, to hear). I notice that
when students begin to tell their own truth they
hesitate, apologize, reveal their uneasiness:*

> ...I write more letters to people now just to
> see if I really can express myself better, and I
> really can. It's a little scary to think a paper
> and pen can do all that. But it is also interest-
> ing in a way....It's like for years now someone
> only let me use a little bit of my brain and now
> in college they gave me the rest of it. Sounds
> weird, huh. But I just can't explain this feeling
> I have...sometimes I feel a little crazy when I
> talk this way.
>
> --Janet Paduaganian

What does it mean to be 20? ...I guess you have
to make the meaning out of it for yourself. To
grow up and become a *man*. I still think of myself as a kid (you know what I mean, not a baby
or an adolescent, but in between that and man-

---

* All excerpts were written by freshmen at the
College of Staten Island.

hood.) Maybe I'm making too big a deal out of
this. Sometimes I get carried away.

                              --Liam Deahl

    My journal started changing when I began to
realize that while no one ever read my journal,
I had an audience. It was a judgmental audience,
a mother-father-teacher me who admonished me before I got a word out: "Put your feelings on paper and they'll be used against you"; "*You* think
that?"; "That's not a very nice thing to say";
and "IF you can't say it right, don't say it at
all." As I became more aware of these voices (that
had always been there, I'm sure), I began to notice
what happened when they spoke. The "bad" thought
did vanish, but so did every other thought; or if
the "proper" thought stayed, I suddenly felt so
bored that I just stopped writing. In short, I
was left with nothing at all. Little by little
I started to talk back to this audience. I
challenged myself to write everything that came
into my mind, no matter how horrible it was, even
if I had to put a blank or an initial in the
place of a word or phrase. With this new rule,
I began to shed my disguises.
    Now the strange thing about disguises in writ-
ing is this: they do cover us when we are afraid
of exposing ourselves, and yet I believe that it
is the desire for openness, for telling things
as they are, that sends us to writing in the
first place. So a person might say, "I want to
write the truth of what's going on with me, but
then I'll have to read it, or maybe someone else
will read it, and everybody, including me, will
see how stupid and messed up I am."
    The fear of exposure is a perfectly reasonable
one in writing. Maybe the material itself is dangerous to look into, or maybe going even a little
below the surface will make a mess that we feel

helpless to put back in order, and then we'll be
left looking stupid. These fears are the territory of writing. Writers who must keep themselves
protected never move far enough into the territory
to get through it. Usually they stay away from
it altogether.

My journal gave me years to try disguise after
disguise, to feel comfortable putting myself on paper, making myself visible, getting closer and
closer to danger. My journal seemed to say to me
all the time, "Just write, go ahead. Don't look
back. There's no need to look back. Use this
journal for what you need now." And what I needed,
and still need, was to be able to say what came
to mind. I needed to have a place where I could
get my own picture of myself, where my honesty
could not disappoint. I needed to have a place
where I had the freedom to speak French, write
my enigmatic poetry, use initials, where I had
time to practice telling the truth that I saw.
What page after blank page said to me was that
here I was trusted, that it was safe here to tell
the truth.

I want my students to have a listener they
can trust the way I had my journal. I want them
to have the experience of acknowledging, in the
company of a quiet listener, the voices they hear,
the details they notice, the inspirations and questions they have.

    ...This class lets you go deep into your mind
  and search for those feelings you were always
  afraid to let out on paper...The students as well
  as the teacher don't try to change your way of
  thinking or even change your style. They just
  give ideas and a way to express yourself more, to
  make your writing better. They try to make your
  writing be you, not something or someone else.

(I hope you understand what I mean. I mean they don't try to make my work into their work.)

--Maria Arnau

I want them to experience writing as a process of reflection.

To me writing reflects your personality. So if you write about something and later read it back, I think you find out a lot about yourself. I remember when I wrote "How I see myself as a writer." What a negative attitude I had. I just couldn't believe it when I read it back to myself. I guess I was ignorant on the subject. That's way I hated it. Now I realize what it (writing) can do for you. You can really see yourself. That's so important to me, knowing who I am and what I want and trying to get it.

--Marianne Remolino

Above all, I want them to see themselves grow in self-awareness and self-confidence, to trust that there never needs to be an end to that growth.

(In September) I was a person with a negative attitude, an infant in writing. Now (in November) I see myself as a two-year-old child. I see and feel myself expanding my thoughts and knowledge in ways I've never done before.

--Joseph Aloi

Sometimes I think about my journals packed in their boxes, sitting at the back of the closet hidden by coats. Sometimes I worry--what if there is a fire? What if they are ever destroyed? What would I do without them? It is strange to have something so valuable that could be destroyed so easily. And yet, the funny thing is, I rarely

reread them. I do not like to go back and read
them. I just keep writing more and more and
seeing more. My journals are a mystery to me.
I cannot figure them out. Why did I start them
in the first place? And yet it is clear to me
that they have been my teacher. They have helped me step out of my disguises and feel the power
of writing. They have been a model to me of the
kind of writing teacher I want to be--patient
and trusting and, like the blank pages, always
expectant and always welcoming.

Richard Elman

STREETS OF THE MOON
      PARIS

Outside the theatre
she glistened in red
plastic like a bomb
about to go off. Her
eyes argued with her
shadow. For a moment
she came toward him
not seeming to notice
the way May heat
seized her by the raincoat
and threw her slicker
image back at the
double glass doors
postered with Roger
Caussimon. Shortly that
amiable large face
would beg him to decide
if he should buy a ticket
to hear of encounters
at Orly Bar, or a
scuzzy weekend lay-
over in Montreal
where they blew their
noses at him
for applause. The life
of a performer
is to be superfluous
just at the right
moments. In the plush
dark loge he oversaw
they were all alone
except for her friend
so blonde she made her
dark hair splendid for

contrasting so much
modishness with his
immodesty. And, afterwards,
in the night she was
beautiful, his goddess
of nothing doing at all
she must be beautiful: Rue
St. Denis smelling
of fog and oysters:

Antoinette, Antoinée...

When I wrote this poem about Paris some years
back, it was inspired by an assignment I'd given
my class in prose fiction: to imagine an unusual
encounter with a stranger, or someone already
known, but under strange circumstances. I can
remember priming them with a passage from Paster-
nak's *Aerial Tracks:* "A single incident brings
you in contact almost for the first time with
the charm of a uniquely significant experience."

As is so often the case when I have been
teaching (and am asked to give specific assignments), I try to fulfill them on my own time.
But it is often difficult for me to write prose
while I'm teaching, whereas the intense experience of a poem comes and passes and can be caught,
if one is at the ready for it. The Paris experience had been real, but I had not thought of it
until I sat down to write. It was like all
flirtations--or nearly so--something that led
nowhere, or almost so, and then it came to me
as these people aware of each other, but from
a great distance, gesturing in the darkness of
a theater.

My students, meanwhile, were engaged in their
own work: a girl from Appalachia, for example,
wrote a brilliant story of a mine strike in

southern Ohio as told by a middle-class woman who, for the first time, becomes aware of her father's complicity in violence.

Another young woman, of middle eastern ancestry, wrote the account of her terrified relatives in the Lebanon of the late '70s, as if she were visiting them from a long way off.

There were stories about meeting Graham Greene, Cord Meyer, Jr., and John O'Hara, and stories about going to visit a friend and running into his crazy wife and/or husband.

Strangest of all, though connected, was the work of a young man of Irish Catholic ancestry, who, having just read Eliot's "Wasteland," described his character standing upon a bridge over a ruined industrial landscape as he explains to his confessor just why he lacked any religious vocation. They also stood apart and did not touch, it seemed to me, like the characters in my poem.

Imitation is often simply pointing oneself this way or that. The flattery is simply in the direction chosen, not in any slavish copying. So it sometimes seems, in the imperfect alchemy we call making art, that a flirtation can become for another writer a discussion of religion. It is no less devout and accepting just because it's not the same.

Harry Greenberg

THE THREE STOOGES AT MY GRANDMOTHER'S FUNERAL

The Stooges did not attend the funeral services,
but they're the first ones to the cemetery.
Moe hugs my father.
Curly walks solemnly down the row of cars
reminding the drivers to turn off their lights.
And Larry chats with my Aunt Sybil,
reminiscing about how her dog Coco
got into the habit of knocking the receiver
off its hook and barking into the phone
every time it rang.
"You know, Syb, we put that piece of business
in our tenth short, *Malice in the Palace*."

The rabbi asks my father to recite
the Mourners' Kaddish with him.
My father's voice drips from his mouth,
in a few moments tears replace his words.
He throws a handful of dirt on the coffin
and it lands in a tight clump.
Moe drops a fistful of dirt into the grave
and whispers, "This is the first time
I've ever thrown dirt at anyone
other than a Stooge. I don't like it."
He helps my father back to the limousine,
both of them weeping like tiny birds.
Larry and Curly shake hands with the rabbi.
The Stooges wave as we pull away.
From far off they flutter and shiver.

This was a difficult poem for me to write. For
most of the afternoon I had seen my father in
tears, his eyes filled with tender memories of

his mother. As we inched our way from the mouth of the grave to a waiting car, his arms wrapped around me for support, I thought of all the times he had offered a steadying hand to my life of abrupt twists and turns. I wanted the poem to articulate my grief at the passing of the woman who gave my dad life and allowed me to choose to sit behind a typewriter. But I went through draft after draft of a poem that had a beginning, a middle, an end, and little else. It conveyed almost nothing of the concern I desired. I was writing from my point of view and I was standing too close.

One day I hit upon the idea of slipping in the Three Stooges, childhood favorites of mine, and having the action swirl around them. Getting them away from their trademarked pokes in the eye and having them behave as caring people caught in tremendous sadness was a startling juxtaposition. I was deeply excited with "The Three Stooges at my Grandmother's Funeral." A delicate situation had been creatively twisted and still managed to capture the compassion I was after.

Around that time I brought in the poem to talk with a fifth-grade class about poetic license--how poets occasionally get material by taking real events and blending in gentle portions of imagination to heighten effects. I explained I do have an Aunt Sybil; she has a crazy dog named Coco; a few people at the funeral forgot to turn their headlights off; my father was in tears and really needed help leaving the cemetery; but the Stooges were only there through the good graces of poetic license. I had no idea that my sharing of this poem would lead to one of the most pleasant experiences I've had teaching.

Greg Raden, a fifth grader in that class who had lost his grandfather the previous summer, privately asked if could work on a funeral poem like mine. I let him know that of course it would be all right, and that if he wanted to talk about it or needed help I would come running. Greg did little writing that class, mostly he rolled his pencil up and down his desk and thought.

The following week I came in with a new lesson. Greg called me over to show he had begun his "funeral" poem at home, but hadn't finished, and wanted to know if I'd permit him to work on it in lieu of the new assignment. I encouraged him to continue, secretly pleased he was sticking with it. One of the toughest things I find to relay to young students is the excitement of revision. To them it is excruciatingly boring to rework material after the initial creative spark has cooled.

Greg was special! He tinkered with every word, crossing out words and squeezing in others. His paper looked like a complicated treasure map with twenty arrows zooming this way and that to mark the spot. Once, he held his poem out to me and said, "How's this so far?" I looked at it for a good two minutes before fessing up, "Greg, I'm having a little trouble fitting all the changes together. It's just great how you're getting your language perfect. You're turning into a true professional. Read it to me now and then make a clean copy before you forget what you want to keep and what you want to take out."

I have never had a student spend so much time on one poem. For three weeks he reworked "The Grandfather Funeral." He knew quite well the feelings and events of that long, sad summer day, but it took a lot of thought to translate the raw hours of that experience to the precious minutes of his poem. Though I never asked him to keep up with the other work covered in class, he did so by doing all the assignments at home. He told me he felt more comfortable

working on his poem in class because we had both
gone through the same ordeal.

His dedication to craftsmanship gave me one
of those "this is what it's all about" moments
we come by all too rarely. Greg had one of
those moments too. When he finished his poem
and read it, everyone in class applauded spon-
taneously. Someone in the back of the room
shouted, "That away, Greg!"

THE GRANDFATHER FUNERAL

I'm in the car
riding to the House of Death
squeezed between relatives
We walk into a dark and lonely room
          with our heads bowed
The rabbi shoves something on my head
I fall into my aunt's arms
My second cousin brings me a drink
A man came out and said,
          "You may come in."
There he lies like a snake in a bottomless
          pit
My mother crying causes a flood
Mine a shower
The lights are dim...So is everyone
The rabbi starts a mournful speech
He mentions my name...I felt proud
We all climb back into cars
"Where are we going?" I asked
"To the cemetery" answers a voice Oh...
I saw a big black car with a wooden box in it
The cars stop
We get out
Stones with names stand tall and broad
We walk under a tent to a big hole in the ground
The box is lowered in
I fall to the ground crying
People start leaving little by little...
They stop by the hole and drop flowers beside it

and drive to my grandmother's
for a feast

Wendy Jones

(Excerpts from "Savannah")

Sundays after church, Jess and I would walk
down Seventh Avenue. My long, thin legs trying
to slow their long pace to Jess' short toddle.
She looked so sweet in her pink organdy dress
starched and pressed, her little Mary Janes with
the buttons on the side of the black patent leather shoes, the pink anklet socks with the frilly
lace at the top and the little white hat with
the pink bow tied in the back just like the
bow tied at what would someday be her waist. I
felt her tiny hand, curled around my index and
middle fingers, damp in the late May warmth.
    "We goin' to Aunt Bannah's, Mama?"
    "Yes, honey. But don't say *we goin'* say
are we going?"
    "Are we *going*? Are *we* going? *Are* we going?"
    She was making my correction into a song,
putting the beat on a different word each time.
I'd given up trying to get her say Aunt Savannah.
It always came out Sabannah which she later
shortened to Bannah, so I just let it stand.
Bannah and Jess got on like white on rice.

> Peas porridge hot
> Peas porridge cold
> Peas porridge in the pot
> Nine days old
>
> Some like it hot
> Some like it cold
> Some like it in the pot
> Nine days old

Without missing a beat, Bannah and Jess clapping
into the next rhyme. Bannah's ham hands stopping

just before patting Jess' miniature ones so the
force wouldn't push her tininess across the
dining room.

> Miss Mary Mack, Mack, Mack
> With silver buttons, buttons, buttons
> All down her back, back, back
> To buy a sack, sack, sack
> And never came back, back, back
> All dressed in black, black, black
> Miss Mary Mack, Mack, Mack

Jess dissolved into giggles in Bannah's lap.
Giggling because she'd one-handed the last "Mack"
instead of two-handing it. She'd made me clap
it out every evening this week so she'd do it
right.
   "Well, Miss Jessie, you almost did it that
time. Alllll most," said Bannah as her gold
rings rubbed the back of Jess' dress.
   "Next time," Jess took her giggles out of
Bannah's lap and floated them toward her face,
the sunlight from the dining room window sparking
the hoops at Bannah's ears with golden fire.
"Next time, I'll get it right!"
   "I bet you will, Miss Jessie, I bet you will,"
Bannah picked Jess up and sat her on her lap.
Jess put her head on Bannah's cushion bosom and
smiled. When she was no more than two, she'd
embarrassed me by saying that when she grew up
she wanted "bumps" just like Aunt Bannah. Bannah
nearly fell off her chair laughing.
   "Careful with your shoes, honey, you'll dir-
ty up Aunt Bannah's pretty white dress." Bannah
always wore white on special occasions. Sunday
was a special occasion.
   "She's all right, Frankie. Yes, Miss Jessie's all *right* with *me*."

●

...Jess went with me to Bannah's house after the
funeral in New York and went down South with us
to the funeral there. As we walked back from
the grave, the South Carolina red dirt baked
hard by a beautiful September sun, she asked me,
"Why wasn't she more careful, Mama? She was always telling *me* to be careful around that window."

"I don't know, Baby. I don't know," I let my
tears come freely. I hadn't cried this much
since Jess' father left. The crying was both
a comfort and a knife in my soul. I'd been
too busy with the funeral arrangements and
helping Bannah's other friends bear up and worrying about Jess to sit down and have my own cry.
And here I was stumbling through red dirt in
high heels, grabbing at Jess' hand because my
tears wouldn't let me see. Bannah, Bannah, why
did you *leave* me?

"Mama, don't cry," Jess patted my hand between her two. "Don't worry. Aunt Bannah's
just sleeping. She'll wake up and we'll play
Mary Mack and I'll get it right this time."

REFEELING

Rewriting is not only the correcting of grammar
and punctuation. Rewriting is *refeeling* the
experience so you can write the emotional truth.

Joanna Emmanuellis is a seventh-grade student
in one of my writing classes. Following is the
first version of her story, "My Dream":

I was walking down a corridor when
I saw a light come from a room. I walked

to the room, but every step I took made the
hallway longer and longer. When I finally
came to the room, I opened the door and suddenly there was a creature, the most horrible
thing in the world! It saw me. I ran as
fast as I could away from it but it caught
up with me. It growled and opened its mouth.
It started putting my head in it. I screamed
and yelled. "I have been eaten and swallowed
by a creature!" I screamed. I opened my
eyes. I was sweating and my fists were
clutching the blanket. After all, this was
just a dream. A horrible dream!

When the class discussed it, they said they
could not *see* the monster. Mr. Talbert, the
class teacher, said he wanted to *feel* what it
was like to be eaten. Joanna's response to the
comments was: "That's too scary!"
"Were you scared when you dreamt it?" I
asked.
"Horribly scared."
I said to the class, "Raise your hand if you
were scared."
No one raised her/his hand.
"Did you want us to be scared?" I asked
Joanna.
"Yes."
"Then you have to be scared when you write
it. You have to take yourself *back* to the feelings and write while sitting *in* those feelings."
What follows is an excerpt from the re-
written version of Joanna's story:

...He growled and opened his mouth. He
started putting my head in it. I screamed
and yelled. He was chewing my flesh up. The
blood was running down his mouth. My head
was in different parts of his mouth and
body. My ears were still in his mouth. One
of my eyes was stuck between his teeth and
the other, who knows where. He was spitting

my teeth on the floor one by one. My nose
was in his throat going down and down to
his stomach. Well, as for my brain and
everything else, I don't know. I opened my
eyes. I was sweating and my fists were
clutching the blanket. After all, this was
just a dream!

When Joanna read *this* to the class, they were *all*
scared.

●

A recent story I rewrote is, like most of my work,
a blend of memory and imagination. "Savannah" is
about the suicide of an older cousin of mine who
was like a mother to my mother and a grandmother
to me. The story traces the emotional connections
between Savannah, known in the latter part of the
story as Bannah, the grown woman and the woman's
little girl.

After my cousin's suicide, I had a continuing series of nightmares about her as horrifying
to me as Joanna's nightmare was to her, but I did
not grieve the way adults do. Years later, I *did*
grieve for another cousin whose death was a jolt-
ing shock. I tried to write a story about my
reactions to his death. When I found I couldn't,
I went back to the earlier death of my older
cousin. I used the feelings of sadness, pain and
anger, which I felt at my young cousin's death, for
"Savannah."

The story told itself best from my mother's
viewpoint. The grieving scene, which is the last
one, was the hardest for me to write. Just as
Joanna did not want to be *scared*, I did not want
to *feel* that *pain*.

In the original version, I was holding back,
trying to protect myself, and cheating the story.
Finally, in the third or fourth draft, the feeling
of anger mixed in with the sadness came back. In

the final rewrite I was able to write the one
sentence that made all the difference to me, the
sentence that made me cry: Bannah, Bannah, why
did you *leave* me?

Kenneth Koch

WEST WIND

It's the ocean of western steel
Bugles that makes me want to listen
To the parting of the trees
Like intemperate smiles, in a
Storm coat evangelistically ground
Out of spun glass and silver threads
When the stars are in my head, and we
Are apart and together, a friend of my youth
Whom I've so recently met--a fragment of the universe
In our coats, a believable doubling
Of the fresh currents of doubt and
Thought! a winter climate
Found in the Southern Hemisphere and where
I am who offers you to wear,
And in this storm, along the tooth of the street,
The intemperate climate of this double frame of the
    universe.

                                    (1954)

(From *The Pleasures of Peace,* Grove, 1969)

TEACHING AND WRITING

The poetry of the children I taught delighted me
and encouraged me, though I think there was more
influence the other way around. I influenced the
children--not by my poems, but by certain ideas
I had about poetry. I assumed that the children
should enjoy writing, be happy and excited while
they were doing it; that their poems didn't
have to intellectually follow but could begin

again and again, change the subject, or go off on
any side way that pleased them; and that the subject of the poem, or, more accurately, what they
wanted to "say," was something they might find
out best while writing, not before. These assump-
tions were good ones, lucky and productive, I
think, for the children's writing, allowing them
to do something they were good at, not something
they were not good at. They were not good at
rhyme and metre, at the rational development of a
subject, at planning a work in advance, at work
that wasn't a pleasure. Here are some of the
poems they wrote:

THE DAWN OF ME

I was born nowhere
And I live in a tree
I never leave my tree
It is very crowded
I am stacked up right against a bird
But I won't leave my tree
Everything is dark
No light!
I hear the bird sing
I wish I could sing
My eyes, they open
And all around my house
The Sea
Slowly I get down in the water
The cool blue water
Oh and the space
I laugh swim and cry for joy
This is my home
      For Ever.

                    --Jeff Morley, 5th grade

COLORS ARE A FEELING

Red makes me feel like sunshine shining on
  a hill.
Blue doesn't look like red. Blue makes the
  day seem dull.
Pink doesn't make me feel like sunshine.
Pink unlike red makes me feel floaty.
Yellow unlike red makes everything around
  me sparkle.
Black makes me feel heavy, very much unlike
  red.
Green makes me feel like I'm all wrinkled
  up.
Green is not as pretty as red, pink or
  orange.
White makes me feel happy just as I am now.
Purple is the end of the day and my poem.

                    --Eliza Bailey, 4th grade

I USED TO BUT NOW

I used to want to be a baseball player with
  my brother
But now I want to be a dancer
I used to want to be a singer
But now I want to be a dancer
I used to want to be a model
But now I want to be a dancer
I used to want to be a queen
But now I want to be a dancer
I used to want to be a dressmaker
But now I want to be a dancer
I used to want to be a boy
But now I want to be a dancer
I used to want to be a pen
But now I want to be a dancer
I used to want to be a king

But now I want to be a dancer

                    --Marion Mackles, 3rd grade

(From *Wishes, Lies, and Dreams,* Chelsea House,
1970 and Harper & Row, 1980)

Giraffes, how did they make Carmen? Well,
    you see, Carmen ate the prettiest rose
    in the world and then just then the
    great change of heaven occurred and she
    became the prettiest girl in the world
    and because I love her.
Lions, why does your mane flame like fire of
    the devil? Because I have the speed of
    the wind and the strength of the earth
    at my command.
Oh Kiwi, why have you no wings? Because I
    have been born with the despair to walk
    the earth without the power of flight
    and am damned to do so.
Oh bird of flight, why have you been granted
    the power to fly? Because I was meant
    to sit upon the branch and to be with
    the wind.
Oh crocodile, why were you granted the power
    to slaughter your fellow animal? I do
    not answer.

                    --Chip Wareing, 5th grade

(From *Rose, Where Did You Get That Red?,* Random
House, 1974)

The lectures I gave and the books I wrote
about teaching children to write poetry did
have some influence on my poems. I think the
introductory essays I wrote for *Wishes, Lies,*

and Dreams and *Rose, Where Did You Get That Red?*
did so particularly. I worked extremely hard on
those introductions. I had never written really
clear expository prose before. Hard as it was,
I began to like it. I began getting aesthetic
sensations from my clear instructional sen-
tences:

> The teacher shouldn't correct a child's
> poems either. If a word or line is un-
> clear, it is fine to ask the child what
> he meant, but not to change it in order
> to make it meet one's own standards. The
> child's poem should be all his own. And
> of course one shouldn't use a child's
> poetry to analyze his personal problems.
> Aside from the scientific folly of so
> doing, it is sure to make children in-
> hibited about what they write.

(From *Wishes, Lies, and Dreams*)

I liked the music that kind of prosy clarity
made, and I wanted to get something like it in
poetry, which I think I did in some of the poems
in *The Art of Love*:

> ...The problem of being good and also doing
>   what one wishes
> Is not as difficult as it seems. It is,
>   however,
> Best to get embarked early on one's dearest
>   desires.
> Be attentive to your dreams. They are usu-
>   ally about sex,
> But they deal with things as well in
>   an indirect fashion
> And contain information that you should have.
> You should also read poetry. Do not eat too
>   many bananas.

In the springtime, plant. In the autumn,
     harvest.
In the summer and winter, exercise. Do not
     put
Your finger inside a clam shell or
It may be snapped off by the living clam...

(From "Some General Instructions," 1974, in
The Art of Love, Random House, 1975)

Phillip Lopate

RUMORS

The whole fifth grade was
suddenly amok with love
Someone had thrown Jonas
against Teresa
in a game of catch-the-girls
And Jonas said I'm sorry
She'd felt her arm slide over his
Next Saturday he took her
to the movies--or so she says
and bought her a bracelet
with two hearts, and
a stuffed felt lion.

Meanwhile David had thrown over
serious-minded Tanya
and showed interest in Wanda,
his former enemy--
after telling everyone
he couldn't stand her guts.
And Wanda knew David's telephone number
by heart.
She told it to her cousin
who called David and said:
What do you think of Wanda?
And David screamed:
I can't stand her guts!
But Wanda knew he'd asked her out
and had to keep their secret
from the world,
and that was just his way.

The others who were not involved
in this romantic life--
the slow ones, the workers,
the short boys--

hated the lovers and called them
brown-noses.
They thought that love meant
sticking one's nose
up a girl's behind.
But Christine, the tall mild grownup
girl who wrote about horses,
thought everyone was acting very childish,
and wondered if the teacher
needed help straightening off
her desk, which looked a mess,
or marking present-and-absent
in the rollbook.

(From *The Daily Round,* SUN, 1976)

MERGING LANES ON A ONE-WAY STREET

The children I worked with changed my life in
many deep ways, but I doubt that they affected
my writing style. I would characterize that
style as analytical and descriptive, focusing
on the psychological and sociological contra-
dictions of daily life. These are modes not too
attractive to elementary school writers, who
gravitate more to the heroic, satiric and super-
natural.* Often, in fact, I envied their sense
of plot. Granted, many of the troubles they in-
flicted on their characters were pinched from

* I need to qualify this generalization by ex-
plaining that occasionally one comes across children who are analytical, who brood ironically
over small discordances in character and who have
a distaste for the heroic. Some of these children
have become my closest friends in the classroom.

television and comic books; but the sheer rapidity with which they pushed their protagonists through a landscape of choice and accident bespoke an affinity for plot at its dizziest, which I could only admire without hoping to imitate. I had been slowed down incalculably by the confusions of life. My aim was to untangle some of the snarls by writing carefully about small moments.

I even tried teaching children a more analytical approach to the moment, to perception and to memory. They did these assignments for me because I asked them to, and because they liked me, but I doubt that it changed their orientation toward the moment. It was more a way of lessening my own feelings of loneliness around them, on those days I felt introverted and cerebral, and longed to be having an adult conversation about Stendhal or Cavafy. Of course, many more times I was delighted to put that introversion aside and be refreshed by their cockeyed surprises. I went into their world of monsters and bandits happily. But sometimes I made them come into my world, just to keep the relationship equitable. Directing a production of Chekhov's *Uncle Vanya* with fifth and sixth graders was one such experiment, as well as a signal to me that I had better get out of working with children soon or I was going to start imposing my own adult ambitions on them in an unhealthy way. Who knows what would have been next: a production of the *Ring* cycle? A Wittgenstein study group?

We PITS (Poets-in-the-Schools) types used to talk about the possible mutual stylistic influences of children's writing and our own. The implication seemed to be that, since we had to make it simple and direct and emotional for children to be attracted to poetry, our own poems would take on these tendencies. Actually, the enormous influence of William Carlos Williams and

the demotic "plain" style on PITS types (as
opposed to poets in the academy) probably came
before any contact with children's writing.
Those drawn into PITS work to begin with were,
on the whole, casual, populist, bohemian and
democratic-sentimental; it's hard to be an aris-
tocratic elitist on that salary or working
with such diverse populations. The bold asser-
tions (sometimes a matter of limited syntactical
repertoire) found so often in children's poetic
lines had a freshness and sincerity not without
comic surrealist undertones, which the PITS-
poet's ear was quick to pick up on, and relish--
though it was more a question of finding support
in an unconscious, largely untutored body of
material for an aesthetic direction one had already started to follow, like Paul Klee letting
the discovery of children's artwork reinforce
his own.

I was bitten as deeply as anyone by the charm
of children's writing, and for a while even pre-
ferred it to the work of my contemporaries in
small press magazines. It felt more "whole,"
since it was less aware or less troubled by what
it had left out; and it certainly felt less
tainted by insecure writer's ego. Nevertheless,
I saw no way to go back to writing like a child.

There were exceptions: an occasional "found"
poem, like "Rumors," in which I basically wrote
down what was happening to a group of fifth
graders in a semblance of their own language
as they had told it to me. Actually, the dic-
tion ended up a mixture of mine and theirs.
I am leery of falling into a *faux-naif* tone,
always a danger in writing about childhood. It
seems to me that an adult writer should never
turn his back on his adult vocabulary. The trick
is to convey the child's psychology in the mature
language and style of the grownup: a double

perspective. When it works, as in *Black Boy,
The Woman Warrior, So Long See You Tomorrow,*
it can be marvelous.

My elementary school students had a deeper
influence on the content of my writing than on
its style. Through the engrossing spectacle of
their lives, they provided me with rich mate-
rial--enough to fill a whole book, *Being With
Children*, and many descriptive articles on education. I also wrote a bad one-act play set
in a children's playground, my one and only
dramatic attempt. I was more sucessful in using
child-characters in my fiction. They appear
prominently in "The Chamber Music Evening" and
a new novella, *The House on the Pond*. There
are also several memoir-essays drawn from my own
childhood in my book, *Bachelorhood*. I think I
would have written these personal reminiscences
of childhood even if I had never taught a single
class, because my childhood haunts me. However,
working with children for twelve years gave me
the confidence to try writing other portraits
of children. I like working with child-characters in family settings because they provide
a relief from the adult longueurs, and represent
a potential for surprise and frankness. They
bounce in and out of the living room so quickly.
You never know what they're going to say in a
scene: Child-characters can be very cute, and
they can also be dangerous, like a ticking bomb.

The debt I owe the children I worked with
is so much larger than I can indicate in this
little essay that it is easier to deny the ways
they might but didn't influence me than to speak
of how they did. This is going to sound sticky,
so to summarize as bluntly as possible: They
made me see that I could be effective in the
world; they made me feel loved; they gave me
faith in my own shaky knowledge that I could

love; and they fed back to me a sense, which had
otherwise always been in doubt, that I was a good
person.

BACKYARD JEALOUSY

It's a hot summer day
and Shelli, like usual, is walking
around showing off with Jennifer.

Hey, Caroline, I say, you wanna play with
me?
I'll tell you who I like.

Okay, you promise you won't tell?
All right.
I think that *Chuckie* is cute.

Well who cares if you don't.
I do!

Look.
There she goes again showing off.
Hey, why are Chuckie and Ricky
chasing Shelli and Jennifer?

Oh. They're playing Run, Catch, and Kiss.
I hate Shelli.
I always knew she was a fake!
I'm never going to play with her again.

Oh. Now they're wrestling on the grass.
Now I hate her
even more.

I'm so jealous.
I don't know why, but I still am.
I feel like crying.
I really do.

Well, I guess I'll go inside and change.
Long pants on a summer day
isn't exactly practical.

I know what.
I'll change into some shorts
and a halter top.
Then maybe Chuckie will notice me.

Oh ya.
I'll put my hair up too.
That's the way Shelli always
does her hair.

There. Hey, Mom!
How do I look?
Thanks, Except I don't want to
take my hair down.

Hey Caroline.
I'm sorry I left you like this.
How do I look?
Thank you.

Let's go play in the playground.

                              --Sarah Oakes, 6th grade

Dick Lourie

SPRING

    (For Cynthia)

I keep saying the details of our lives
are also our symbols and our mysteries
but people don't always believe it

I felt all this again today sitting
in your house: it's early March R has
  come
from Chicago to visit you and your
woods fifty miles from New York City

I keep trying to simplify my life
opening windows closing doors
attacking the papers on my desk as
if they were the sad story of all my
lovers this winter taking up the space
I need to write new poems

you stop work on your novel about strangers
and put us all in a new piece of which
you are directly the center and it
keeps happening to itself as you keep
sticking in the events of five minutes ago

V has written you from Berkeley that the
baby he delivered in the snow-bound
mountain cabin last December has died
unwanted we are all wondering what
we want besides the new chance at spring

my weeks ahead are filled with work at
  schools
that want poets to shine on their kids
  now the

snow's gone: in May you'll head for New
  Mexico
R will be back in Chicago I'll be
here waiting for C to come visit from
Milwaukee maybe all three of you will
by accident meet on the road for coffee

our friendship is blooming again you and
I between the two of us we may get
around enough to carry the smells of
spring almost anywhere sometimes I
really feel years as they say fall away
and time that invention yielding to the
seasons of earth

I have never used my poem "Spring" as a
model in the classroom, but I think that
what I have to tell kids, what I want to
show them about the relationship between
life and art, is pretty well expressed in
the poem's first two lines. A good many
of my poems are entirely literal, and
sometimes entirely factual, akin to docu-
mentary photography or filmmaking. I
don't use metaphor very much in my poems.
It has always seemed important to me to
show students that the literal has as much
place in poetry as the metaphorical.
      Needless to say, I don't claim to have
invented this idea. The influences on my
own early work, those writers whose poems
impelled me toward the kind of writing
that has evolved into my "style" (or at
least my way of looking at things), were
Whitman and Williams, both of whose work
I do use as models in the classroom.

One of the things I find most often when
I go into a school is teachers as well as kids
believing that for something to be counted as
"creative" it has to be made up--and the less re-
semblance to real life the better. I myself long
ago stopped using the term "creative," since it
invariably leads to such misunderstanding. I
always tell students that we are going to do "imaginative" writing. Like "image," I say, imagining
refers to the capability of picturing something in
your head--whether it's real or not--and so
"imaginative" is a more inclusive term than
"imaginary."

Often what I ask my students to do first of
all is to imagine something real, like their room
at home, using Williams' "Nantucket" as a model
(thanks to a suggestion by poet Bob Hershon).
Then they imagine what someone they know might be
doing right this minute--get it written down so
we can see it, I tell them. I call this a "movie"
poem, and the models for it are usually poems by
other kids. After they are able to concentrate
enough to visualize a person who's not there, and
to follow his/her activities in their minds for
five minutes, I figure they can concentrate enough
to actually watch people, so I send them somewhere
to do that.

In effect, this introductory procedure gives
a lot of practice in turning the details of the
world into poems, exercising a high degree of
selectivity, with a minimum of invention. The
length of residencies most places being what it
is (with T&W as a blessed exception), I rarely get
much beyond this first level of responding to the
world by representing some aspect of it with
accuracy and detail. But this seems to me a suf-
ficiently important activity in itself.

When I worked with 5th and 6th graders at the
Robert Frost (by coincidence) Elementary School in

East Brunswick, New Jersey, we had a longer time than usual to get acquainted and work on poems. We did do metaphor, and various other things, but the most exciting aspect of this residency for me was the "room poems" and the "movies," and their variant, "slow-motion" poems in which you describe someone for about 30 seconds--our model was Williams' poem about the cat and the jamcloset.

I suggested to the kids that they copy their poems on newsprint, big, so we could fill a hall-way with them, very noticeably, for everyone to see and read. These room poems and movie poems and slow-motion poems were as plain as the newsprint, for the most part. Also, they were un-adorned by any illustration and, if the truth be told, they were not very elegantly calligraphed (is that a verb?). It was like life being turned into words, but with no fuss and little delay. I saw my friend Cynthia's short story: "it keeps happening to itself."

In at least one instance at Frost the corres-pondence was between the poem and the life of the school. After a lot of practice imagining, I sent two of my star fifth graders down to the school cafeteria one morning to observe and then to write movie poems describing the pre-lunch, lunch, and post-lunch activities.

As it happens, Frost School has one of the best cafeterias going. The food is not bad, and the staff is a lively bunch. They always carry on their jobs with real verve (I don't use that word often), and they have a good time. Cheryl Domenichetti's poem featured lines like "Helen is cleaning up trays while the rest argue with Jenny because she doesn't want to answer the phone." Jonathan Ackerman wrote: "The milk lady strolls out her cart...."

When these were copied out big, we brought them to the cafeteria, and the ladies hung the poems up on their kitchen wall, where they stayed until we had our public reading later in the spring.

This event featured everyone in the class reading at least one poem. As a display, we set up portable bulletin boards, and hung all the big-print poems, so the parents could walk among them as in a gallery. You could see they were impressed, although they were not too sure what this had to do with poetry. Like most other people, they wanted to think of poems as very removed from life, not very involved with life (let me refer you now to the *third* line of my poem). But the kids had all got the point, which was the very simple one that *their* lives could generate art, and that the making of a poem could be a matter of selection as well as invention. My students understood that they had both the resources and the power to make poetry.

During the course of the evening, I think the parents also came to understand, because they saw their daughters and sons coming to the microphone one by one and reading poems that *were* made from their own lives, and yet, like art, transcended the moments of experience they were drawn from, through that process of distillation that is so easy to recognize and so hard to describe.

I was proud of the kids and of my own efforts as well. They in turn were proud of their poems and the over-sized copies that showed them off. We all had a fine evening, and if I hadn't already written those first lines of "Spring," I'm sure I could have done it right then.

Clarence Major

LOWER EAST SIDE: 1960's

I want to try
to be fair about this.
So far I haven't been.
To the left is a dark woman
with long black hair.
Dressed in a white cotton shirt
and a long blue cotton skirt.
So there.

What good does it do?
I could explain--describe--
everybody on the street
and even the physical relation
of each
to each in the frame. Of
the eye. The fruit and vegetable
carts and the old horses.
The cries the talk the laughter.
The fast-talking foreign accents.
Blankets and sheets
hanging from second story fire escapes.
I did want to trail the scene.
Fast and smoothly. But
I lived here too long
without knowing them.

INTERVIEW WITH CLARENCE MAJOR

(This is an excerpt from an interview that took
place in Boulder, Colorado on March 18, 1981.)

NANCY BUNGE: You've said things that imply to me that you believe in order to write anything original or interesting, you have to get as close to your perception of things as you can.

CLARENCE MAJOR: I don't remember saying that, but it sounds true. (*Laughter*) I would say that it's very complex and difficult because this whole idea of getting into yourself constitutes a problem because if you're writing from an intensive, personal, subjective point of view, you're also facing the inevitable problem of near-sightedness. You're very likely to miss something. One example: I was living in New York. I was walking along the street and passing in front of the laundromat and a dog was tied to the parking meter. A little girl came out of the laundromat to pet the dog and the dog bit off her ear. Whack! Just like that. A lot of people gathered around and it was a very tragic moment. It was not the thing you would expect on a casual afternoon; people were feeling good in the city; it was one of the first warm days. I tried to write a poem about it. I wanted to say something about how it affected me and what the implications were: how unsafe I felt we all were, forever. To try to put that on paper proved to be extremely difficult and finally, impossible. I was just too close to it. I tried to do it that very day. What we very often need is some distance, not just from the experience, but from ourselves, in order to write anything worthwhile.

That distance is very necessary and can be achieved in different ways. Usually my process is doing a first draft and not knowing how I feel about it. I'll put it away and look at it six months later, three weeks later, sometimes two years later, and then I can start working at the thing in some sort of objective way, because I can then

see what's there in a way that I wasn't able to
see in the beginning. But that's my process. I
tend to overwrite and have to cut a lot, so usually what I do is look for the essence of it and
try to refocus the thing and glean out whatever
vitality might be there. But I don't necessarily
encourage my students to write that way. We're
all individuals, and we're all different. There
are many, many ways in which things can be accom-
plished. What I try to do is understand my students' processes. It's really interesting for me
to see all those different ways that things can
be made, watching the students work.

NB: So you try to understand how they go about it
and then reinforce whatever...

CM: Yeah, right. And I don't ever impose a group
assignment, but I make assignments optional so
that they pick and choose because the students
work in different ways, and it would be unreason-
able to try to make all them in my image.

NB: Or encourage them to do anything in a certain way.

CM: Right. Except their way.

NB: That must be exhausting.

CM: It is, it is. (*Laughter*)

NB: Someone else I've spoken with said that his
students think that all good writing makes an
important point and so they spend all their
energy trying to think up a "significant thesis."
Have you seen that tendency in your students?

CM: Yes, especially the fiction writers. They
have an argument that they need to give expression

to, and they build the story around the argument.
There is a student in one of my classes now who
writes excellent satirical pieces about political
situations, and you can see that the fiction is
really there as a kind of conveyor for this argument. Well, then you think, that's what the
history of satire has always been, really. You
look back to Swift; you look back to Nathaniel
West. I think it's OK and probably works pretty
well, and it certainly has a substanial tradition.
But the other situation is a lot more aggravating:
where the students have some sort of muddled notion of what the point of view should be and so
on and simply try to decorate that idea with a
few pages of careless prose. That's a lot more
disturbing from my point of view.

NB: What do you do?

CM: I do several things, depending on the situation. (*Laughter*) I try the positive approach, to
use these pieces in different ways to discuss
writing problems. But I run into the problem of
so many students being in workshops for approval
rather than tough, hard criticism, and that's one
of the more difficult things that I have to face
in dealing with the kinds of manuscripts that
are, quote--not worth talking about--unquote.
    I don't believe that I can always help any-
one become a better writer, but I think I can
always help them become better readers and then
become more sensitive to the language and how it's
put together. They take that writerly experience
back to the reading process; I've seen it happen.
They understand something of the process and therefore they can read with greater sensitivity, and
more pleasure too.

NB: A large number of the people I've spoken with
talk about the importance of having their students
read aloud and listen to their own work. Is that...

CM: Yeah, I think so. I have certain kinds of
prose read in class because they lend themselves
to that kind of expression; it's not just a
visual experience. I certainly learn a lot by
reading my work in public; it's a way of educating
myself in public, or not educating myself, but
rewriting, which is an educational process. And
a way of getting distance too, looking at my work
from different angles. Very often right in front
of an audience, I will make a mental note to
change something I'm reading because I've suddenly
had the experience of seeing what's wrong with it
as I'm reading it. So I think reading aloud is
important.

NB: One article I read suggested having the students talk into tape recorders and then write
from that material. The author said he thought
that would make what they wrote more honest because people tend to lie when they write.

CM: They think of writing only as an approximation of their speech and the extent of our normal experience with writing is to write a letter
to someone and it's not really the same. It's
always the same tired, worn-out expressions:
"Dear Betty, I'm sorry that I didn't write earlier...," rather than doing it the way we would
speak. We get into the habit of thinking that
writing cannot be an instrument of the speaking
voice, but the most effective writing has been
an approximation of the voice. I'm always trying
to get students to write in their own voices and
also to write out of their experiences and to
write about what they know about and part of that
process involves using an approximation of their
own speech, not the way Shakespeare wrote and
talked.

NB: That sounds good. I had a student last year

who used inflated language, because he was scared,
I guess, and when he came to my office, I had
him read his paper out loud. He knew right away
what the problem was.

CM: I run into it all the time with students who
will get fascinated with a certain writer and
they'll be writing that writer's prose. That's
fine as a learning process, but one should move beyond that and constantly think in terms of moving
toward one's own voice and one's own speech and
one's own rhythms. That idiom is a vital part of
the experiences they should be writing about.
   Most students in college today aren't going to
have an opportunity to be in touch with who they
are and where they come from in such an intense
way ever again as they will in a workshop. They
will go into different kinds of things: business,
engineering, the sciences; but, hopefully, they
will remember how important it was to create a
wedding of the voice that was theirs and the history that was theirs. No matter how much television one watches or how many movies one watches,
the kinds of associations produced by those kinds
of experiences remain marginal and accidental and
incidental; they won't be like the experience of
writing and discovering one's voice and creating
that bridge to an audience. That's an entirely
unique experience that there is no substitute for.

Miguel Ortiz

THE COAT

When it snowed my brother and I watched from our
window. Roofs, antennas, skylights all turned
white.
     "I don't want to go out by myself," Norberto
said.
     "You have to. We can't both go together. I'll
watch you through the window."
     We had to ask permission.
     "Ma!" I shouted. She was in the other room
ironing. "Can Norberto go out in the snow, then
me?"
     "Yes," she said. "But don't cross the street."
He put on the coat. It was a brown coat with a
checkered pattern running from the shoulders to the
waist on both sides of the front. It was an old
coat that had belonged to one of our cousins. Some
of our cousins had been born in New York. We had
never seen them before. When we came it was
October, not very cold. My father, who had been
here already for six months, met us at the airport.
He had jackets for us, and they were all right
because it was not winter yet. We visited all
our cousins we had never seen before, and when the
winter came one of them gave us a coat, but there
were two of us.
     He went out. I watched for him through the window
Below was an empty lot. The snow was falling,
piling up on the window ledge. I opened the window a little, gathered the white powder into a
ball and tossed it from hand to hand. My fingers
became red, so I put the snow down on the window
sill. I looked out on the white world. It was
silent. Everything seemed numb. Norberto appeared
in the lot. He raised his hands over his head and
waved them back and forth. He was shouting something at me, but I couldn't hear him. He ran

around, twice stopping to shake the show from his
shoes. He made a snowball and threw it against
a brick wall. Then he disappeared around the edge
of the building toward the stoop.

Soon he was back.

"It's too cold," he said. "My feet are freez-
ing."

"I got some snow from the window," I said. I
turned to get the snowball. There was a puddle
on the window sill. Water was dripping on the
floor.

"You better clean it up," he said, glancing
toward the other room.

I got the dish rag from the sink and was
wiping up the snow water when my mother walked in.
She didn't say anything. I waited.

"How's the snow?" she asked Norberto.

"Too cold, " he answered. "My feet got wet."

"Put on a dry pair of socks," she said. She
sat him down on a chair and took off his shoes and
socks. She rubbed his feet to make them warm.

"Are you going out too, Mario?" she asked.

"Yeah, I want to see what it's like."

"It's cold!" Norberto said.

"Get something from the store," she said.

"All right," I said.

She didn't say anything about the water. She
told me what to get. Norberto handed me the
coat.

"Here's the notebook," my mother said. I
reached out for the notebook and put it in the
coat pocket. It was a little notebook.

I went out. The radiator in the hallway, under the battered mailboxes, was knocking like
crazy. I hurried into the street.

The snow was coming down very thick. The foot
prints my brother had made were almost covered.
There were no people on the street except for me.
I waited on the stoop wondering what to do. I
looked up to let the snow fall on my face. Snowflakes melted on my nose and cheeks. I made a

snowball and threw it at a parked car, then looked
around to check whether anyone had seen me.

It was no fun to be alone. I ran a little
way on the sidewalk then looked back to see my
tracks. I walked backward stepping in my foot-
prints. It looked as if I had disappeared where
my tracks stopped. That was an Indian trick I had
seen in a comic book. I had a seen a lot of things
in comic books. 'Specially comic books about
Indians. Suppose an Indian wanted a coat. He'd
go out in the woods, hunt down a bear, take the
skin and make himself a bear skin coat. First
he'd look for tracks, then dig a hole right where
the tracks are because that's where the bear walks
He'd cover the hole with branches, so that it looks
like there's no hole there at all. When the bear
comes by, swapo! Right into the trap. I wished
I could hunt down a bear for a coat. I went in
the empty lot, and I started to dig a hole in the
snow. I knew there weren't any bears in New York
City, but there was nothing else to do. I looked
up to the window. Norberto was there.

"I'm gonna catch a bear," I shouted up to him,
pointing at the hole.

He put his hand to his ear. I shouted louder.
He shook his head, his hand still at his ear. He
couldn't hear me. I wished that he were helping
me to dig the hole. But then if he were with me
there wouldn't be any need to catch a bear. I got
to thinking that since there were no bears, probably the only thing that would fall in the hole
would be a stray dog. That wouldn't be any good
for a coat.

Digging a hole in snow was hard work, and I
had no gloves and no galoshes. I couldn't tell
which were colder, my hands or my feet. I remembered the store. The wind had started up, and the
snowflakes were wild, running in waves as if to
escape but only dashing themselves against cars
and walls, then falling to the ground.

In back of the grocery store there was a little
bell that was attached to the door by a string.
Whenever anyone came in through the front, the bell
rang, to let Don Justino, the grocer, know that
someone was in. That way if anybody came to rob
him, he wouldn't be caught by surprise. Besides
the bell Don Justino had a German shepherd that
growled all the time. It had attacked Don Justino
once. I remember Don Justino had bandages all over
his face and hands, but he still kept the dog. I
guess he was more afraid of losing his money than of
being mauled, though he did put a muzzle on the
dog after that. Beside the store Don Justino owned
a brick house and a row of garages, which he
rented out, behind the house. Everyone bought on
credit at Don Justino's, and he even lent out money. He was always writing down numbers. He would
write in his big book how much you owed him, and he
would write down in your little book how much you
owed him. And sometimes people would just say a
number to him, and he would write it down in a
different book. I didn't know then why he did that.
On Sundays he gave away money to policemen. That
was, my father said, so he might sell beer on a
day meant for going to church.

The bell rang when I walked into the store.
Some of the snow tried to get in with me.

"*Dos libras de arroz y una caja de abichuelas,*"
I said to Don Justino.

There were candy jars on the counter. They sat
there grinning like fat little men. The jellybean
jar laughed a rainbow of jellybean colors that
broke up into perfect jellybeans. The more it
laughed the more jellybeans appeared. Then they
fell on the counter making a sound like raindrops
on a window pane.

"Anything else?" Don Justino asked.

The jellybeans disappeared.

I handed him the little notebook. He wrote
down how much we owed him for the rice and beans.

Another kid walked in with a notebook just like mine.

"Isn't that your brother's coat?" he said.

I didn't say anything, but he said, "You wanna come out later to play?"

"I don't know," I said. "My name is Mario. My brother's name is Norberto."

"I'm Raymond. Your brother can't come. He don't have no coat. "

I didn't say anything.

WRITING AND TEACHING

How does teaching affect the writer's writing? When I first approached the job, I didn't have a clear overview of the matter. I was confronted with a roomful of students who were supposed to write in my presence. I thought my task was to provide assignments that would serve as catalysts. We can call this the Firecracker Approach: The students are charged but inert until the fuse is lit, at which point they explode with creativity. This was the prevalent approach in the late '60s. All the T&W writers were busy creating starter exercises, the kind in *The Whole Word Catalogue 1*. This approach worked well enough at the time. But I began to ask myself, "Is this the way I write?" I couldn't tell my students just to wait until inspiration strikes. That was what I did in my own writing. But it was too unrealistic for the classroom.

I had no satisfactory way of solving this dilemma, but I had become alerted to the fact that I needed answers. I tried to remember exactly what I did when I sat down to write: my mind would usually become unfocused for a while. Some-

times an image would appear, and I would jot it
down. Sometimes I'd have intimations of a rhythm,
and I'd try to find words to fit it. But sometimes my mind remained unfocused, and I was un-
able to write anything.

I picked up clues where I could. I read
books about writing. I kept a sharp eye out
for what other writer/teachers were doing. I
tried using a tape recorder with children. That
turned out to be an excellent tool in the classroom. I tried it on myself--no go. I could
not compose on the machine. Writing had to be
something more than speech.

Finally I hit upon a plausible model of the
mental activities that lead to writing. I pre-
supposed that the mind is constantly generating
streams of words and images that relate to whatever input it has ever received. Since sensory
input is myriad, we may assume that there are
multiple and simultaneous generations of words
and images. The generating mechanism may be like
a magic cauldron that bubbles continually, the
contents never diminishing no matter how much of
it is siphoned off. The problem of writing then
becomes one of creating the siphon and seeing to
it that only the appropriate material flows
through it. So the problem often thought of as
scarcity (the proverbial "dry spell") may really
be one of access to overabundance.

This view of the origins of the writing stream
has made me feel certain that the basic material
is there, and it has removed a great deal of
anxiety from the process of setting it down. The
less anxiety there is, the easier it becomes to
order the material, because the act of focusing
becomes more manageable. Teaching writing forced
me to analyze my own writing process, and I eventually came away with an understanding of it that
led to better writing for me.

I doubt that through my contact with the
students I experienced some subtle alteration of

writing consciousness. Although children's lack of sophistication often allows them to use language in a startling way (which many poets strive to do), this ability in children is due primarily to a lack of facility with the language rather than a mastery of it. When my three-year-old son describes an eye ailment by saying, "I have a bicycle wheel in my eye," it is to him an accurate description of how his eye feels, not an attempt to be figurative. As his vocabulary increases he is likely to abandon the image of the bicycle wheel because it will no longer seem to him accurate enough. Many of us who have worked in the schools have been inclined to look at this progression in children-- from what appears to be figurative language to more abstract forms-- as a corruption brought about by education. In truth it is a natural development. It seems to us a falling from grace, because as sophisticated adults we are moving in the opposite direction. We are trying to hone our ability to produce figurative language, and so we envy what seems effortless in the child. What the child is doing is not really what we want to do, though on the surface it is strikingly similar.

In the final analysis, the influence of teaching on my writing was not so much external--not from the students as much as from myself. The classroom experience forced me to fall back on my own experience with writing, and in that way I was unavoidably confronted with the persistent problems of creating order out of chaos, which is essentially what writing is about.

Abiodun Oyewole

ANOTHER MOUNTAIN

Sometimes there's a mountain
  that I must climb
even after I have climbed one already

But my legs are tired now
and my arms need a rest
my mind is too weary right now
But I must climb before the storm comes
before the earth rocks
and an avalanche of clouds buries me
and smothers my soul
And so I prepare myself for another climb
Another mountain
and I tell myself it is nothing
it is just some more dirt and stone
and every now and then I should reach
another plateau and enjoy the view
of the trees and flowers below
And I am young enough to climb
and strong enough to make it to any top
You see the wind has warned me
about settling too long
about peace without struggle
The wind has warned me
and taught me how to fly
But my wings only work
After I've climbed a mountain

In a world of color televsion, quadrophonic sound cinemas, 2000 lb. portable radios, stereos, super Sony Walkmans, newspapers, magazines, billboards, telegrams and mailgrams, "word of mouth" still reigns supreme. Oral tradition still remains the most viable and effective means of communication.

For the last three years I have used an oral tradition concept to teach children and young adults creative writing. For example, if I want to teach simile I sing one of my original songs that highlights the use of simile: "Just like the leaves holding on in a breeze we got to be strong and get along" ("Black Order"). This both illustrates my point and gets juices flowing by having everyone sing along.

It is important to note however that in order for this oral tradition approach to teaching to be successful, the teacher has to memorize numerous poems and songs as well as have the ability to perform them. With this approach each class session is like a performance with audience participation. With the recent advent of the "Rap"--a rhyming story done to a disco beat-- this concept becomes even more viable and valuable.

Many teachers and parents have complained to me that all their kids do is repeat those "stupid" raps all day, such as the Sugar Hill Gang's "Hotel motel Holiday Inn if your girl starts acting up then you take her friend."

Even though I had taught children the poetry of Langston Hughes and Mari Evans, as well as other children, none of this had the force of the Sugar Hill Gang or Master Flash and the Furious Five. I began realizing it wasn't so much the words, that came at you at the speed of light in a most incoherent fashion, it was the rhythm--the percussion of the rhyme and the sensuality of the human voice pulsating in an intense rhythm supported by loud percussion in-

struments--that created this force. Many times
I've asked the kids what these groups are saying
and to explain it to me. They seem almost
amazed because it's something they've never
thought about before. They just repeat the raps
like a well-programmed computer.

With this new knowledge, I began bringing
in "consciousness raising" raps. For example:
"Now is the time for us to be more in control of
our destiny / change the game from rich and poor
and learn to love each other more," (from my
rap poem "Now Is The Time").

Another aspect of rap poetry that coincides
with good ol' oral tradition is the concept of
storytelling. In most cases a story is being told
in rap poems, rhythm 'n' blues songs and even in
some disco. The story is not always the most
positive or mentally stimulating, but there are
stories nonetheless.

In addition to the percussive rhythm and
the story, there is a special vocabulary common
to each generation. There are certain slang
expressions like "That's Badd" and "Take a chill
pill" that become an integral part of the com-
munications network among young people.

In my efforts to communicate with the young
folks, I used one of their popular slang expressions, "I got it like that" (an expression
that exudes confidence), to develop a story-
poem which later became a song about a young man
trying to court a girl who looks physically mature but is in fact only in her early teens. In
the song I used figurative language as well as
the three main ingredients of oral tradition:
strong rhythm and rhyme, storytelling, and language common to the people.*

* "She Got It Like That" is available from
Street Beat Records.

One of the most incredible results of my
teaching oral poetry is that the children in the
upper grades voluntarily share the songs and poems
with the children of the lower grades. This is
what the oral tradition is all about. Academi-
cally, the definitions of poetry, prose, and all
of their ingredients (metaphor, simile, allitera-
tion, personification, and onomatopoeia) are understood better because the students now have tangible examples in original songs and poems, some
by the children themselves.

●

Harlem is like a red rose
Harlem is like a book with black and white pages
Harlem is like a magic potion
Harlem is like a pot of black eye peas
Being in Harlem is like kissing someone you love

                    --Karen Haskett

●

Harlem is like a black and white T.V.
Harlem is like the blackest night
Harlem is like a red black and green rainbow
Harlem is sweet like a chocolate cake
Sometimes Harlem is like a wild woolly cat

                    --Latasha Matthews

●

Harlem is like a bell
Sometimes it's like a wishing well
Harlem's got a nice smile
and a whole lot of style

                    --Victor Tuck

Ron Padgett

HIGH HEELS

I have a vision
in my head of Cubism
and Constructivism
in all their artistic purity
joined with a decorative attractiveness
that exceeds deliciousness,
even more to be desired
than becoming a milkman
in a white suit and hat
delivering milk to the back door
of a white frame house
on a street lined with elms
and being invited inside
by the curvaceous, translucent lady
of the house, not once
but many times, too many times,
perhaps, for later her husband
will be coming home
with a sledgehammer in his hand,
the pink hand with light blue fingernails, oh
you have colored the wrong picture!
You were to put the pink and blue
on the beachball on the next page.

(From *Triangles in the Afternoon*, SUN, 1979)

THREE LITTLE WORDS

The mountain grew
as the winding road cracked
and the bird watched.

The boob had continuing excitement
with a typewriter on fire.

The cornucopia filled with colored popcorn
tumbled onto the map of Fredonia.

The enormous Yugoslavian has no cartilege.

The peachy tomatoes fell on the oceanographer's
   head.

We played baseball and the temperature
   was rising like the people.

                              --Collaboration, 11th grade

I once had an odd experience in the classroom.
Or rather, one of my students did.
      It was in Newark, Delaware, spring of 1975.
I was in the final week of teaching poetry in all
the city's junior high schools for three months,
five days a week. At that point I was really
rolling, from both the exhilaration of knowing
that I had enjoyed such a demanding residency and
from the sheer momentum of sustained high-energy
teaching. I was having especially good teaching
experiences in working with dreams and dreamlike
material. There was something about the children
in Newark that made them very excited about thinking and talking and writing about their dreams,
as if they had been waiting all their lives for
this chance.
      Those three months I kept a diary, using a
tape recorder. Every morning, at first dim
consciousness, I recounted my dreams into the
bedside microphone, usually without opening my
eyes. And every afternoon after work I described

the day's teaching experiences. So the diary went dream/teaching/dream/teaching/etc. My dreams appeared to be unaffected by my teaching, but my teaching took on something like the automatic magic of the dream. Simply telling my dreams to the students, for "starters," put some weird fascination into the air.

In this particular class--a bright and responsive one--I started by talking about dreams and nightmares, dreams continuing after you fall back asleep, recurring dreams, déjà vu, how to remember your dreams better, how to influence them to some extent, what dreams might mean, and some of the ways they work, especially how they mysteriously transpose places and people and times, and how the dreamer can be both in a dream and outside it at the same time. About then I noticed that a girl sitting in the back had begun to cry silently, but rather than call attention to her I kept talking, as the teacher tactfully escorted her out.

The next day I was told that the girl had been taken to the nurse's office, where she had sobbed and muttered incoherently for 20 minutes. She then calmed down enough to tell her best friend that during the class *she had seen her grandmother enter the room, walk over, hand her a cat, and then exit, and that she knew with absolute certainty then that her grandmother had just died*. Aside from this experience of an unexpected visitation, the girl was thought to be normal.

I single out this experience not because I think its strange unhappiness is desirable, but because it serves as a graphic (if gloomy) parallel to what I sometimes experience when writing poetry: the words arrive unexpectedly in my mind and flow down through my fingers onto the page, taking sudden turns on their own. It is similar to--but not the same as--automatic writing, for although I relinquish some control of the poem, I do monitor its arrival. I even feel free enough

to allow my aesthetic judgement to move in and
out of the poem, altering the poem's automatic
turns almost as they happen.

For example, in "High Heels" the abstract
music of the first six lines--the sonority of
those words read aloud or heard in the mind--
gives way suddenly to a pleasant visual image
from a late 1930s movie, which then becomes
threatening with the idea of the angry husband,
and then comic with the exaggeration of "sledgehammer." Abruptly the camera zooms in on the
husband's hand, the outline of a hand from a
coloring book, and even more suddenly--with the
"oh"--a different voice is saying the poem's
last three lines. And then the voice is gone:
the poem is over.

This poem burst in on me one night and took
three minutes to be written. I don't know where
it came from, but I do know that it's mysteriously
satisfying to write poems such as "High Heels."
I wanted my students to have something of that
experience, too, so--sometimes at the risk of
being the boob with his flaming typewriter--I
designed writing situations for them in which the
everyday world reveals something surprising and
true about itself or else just falls away completely.

Grace Paley

•

A woman invented fire and called it
                    the wheel
Was it because the sun is round
        I saw the round sun bleeding to sky
And fire rolls across the field
        from forest to treetop
It leaps like a bike with a wild boy riding it

oh   she said
            see the orange wheel of heat
light   that turned me from the
        window of my mother's home
to home in the evening

SOME NOTES ON TEACHING:
Probably Spoken

Here are about fifteen things I might say in the
course of a term. To freshmen or seniors. To
two people or a class of twenty. Every year the
order is a little different because the students'
work is different, and I am in another part of my
life. I do not elaborate on plans or reasons, because I need to stay as ignorant in the art of
teaching as I want them to remain in the art of
literature. The assignments I give are usually
assignments I've given myself, problems that
have defeated me, investigations I'm still pur-
suing.

1. Literature has something to do with language. There's probably a natural grammar at the
tip of your tongue. You may not believe it, but

if you say what's on your mind in the language
that comes to you from your parents and your
street and friends you'll probably say something
beautiful. Still, if you weren't a tough recal-
citrant kid, that language may have been destroyed
by the tongues of schoolteachers who were ashamed
of interesting homes, inflection, and language
and left them all for correct usage.

2. A first assignment: To be repeated whenever necessary, by me or the class. Write a
story, a first person narrative in the tongue of
someone with whom you're in conflict. Someone
who disturbs you, worries you, someone you don't
understand. Use a situation you don't understand.

3. No personal journals, please, for about
a year. Why? Boring to me. When you find only
yourself interesting, you're boring. When I find
only myself interesting, I'm a conceited bore.
When I'm interested in you, I'm interesting.

4. This year, I want to *tell* stories. I
ask my father, now that he's old and not so busy,
to tell me stories, so I can learn how. I try
to remember my grandmother's stories, the faces
of her dead children. A first assignment for
this year: Tell a story in class, something that
your grandmother told you about a life that pre-
ceded yours. That will remind us of our home
language. Another story: at Christmas time or
Passover supper extract a story from the oldest
persons told them by the oldest persons they remember. That will remind us of history. Also--
because of time shortage and advanced age, neither
your father or your grandmother will bother to
tell unimportant stories.

5. It's possible to write about anything in
the world, but the slightest story ought to contain the facts of money and blood in order to be
interesting to adults. That is--everybody continues on this earth by courtesy of certain economic arrangements, people are rich or poor, make a
living or don't have to, are useful to systems, or

superfluous. --And blood--the way people live as
families or outside families or in the creation
of family, sisters, sons, fathers, the bloody ties.
Trivial work ignores these two FACTS and is never
comic or tragic.

     May you do trivial work?

WELL

    6. You don't even *have* to be a writer.
Read the poem "With Argus," by Paul Goodman. It'll
save you a lot of time. It ends:

> The shipwright looked at me
> with mild eyes.
> "What's the matter friend?
> You need a New Ship
> from the ground up, with art,
> a lot of work,
> and using the experience you
> have--"
> "I'm tired!" I told him in
> exasperation,
> "I can't afford it!"
>   "No one asks you, either,"
> he patiently replied, "to venture
> forth.
> Whither? why? maybe just forget it,"
> And he turned on his heel and left
> me--here.

    7. Lucky for art, life is difficult, hard to
understand, useless and mysterious. Lucky for
artists, they don't require art to do a good day's
work. But critics and teachers do. A book, a
story, should be smarter than its author. It is
the critic or the teacher in you or me who cleverly
outwits the characters with the power of prior
knowledge of meetings and ends.

    Stay open and ignorant.

    (For me, the problem: How to keep a class of
smart kids--who are on top of Medieval German and
Phenomenology--dumb? Probably too late and impossible.)

Something to read: Cocteau's journals.

8. Sometimes I begin the year by saying:
This is a definition of fiction. Stesichorus was
blinded for mentioning that Helen had gone off to
Troy with Paris. He wrote the following poem and
his sight was restored:

> Helen, that story is not true
> You never sailed in the benched ships
> You never went to the city of Troy.

9. Two good books to read:

> A *Life Full of Holes*, Charhadi
> I *Work Like a Gardener*, Joan Miro

10. What is the difference between a short
story and a novel? The amount of space and time
any decade can allow a subject and a group of
characters. All this clear only in retrospect.
Therefore: Be risky.

11. A student says--why do you keep saying
a Work of Art? You're right. It's a bad habit.
I mean to say a Work of Truth.

12. What does it mean To Tell the Truth?
It means--for me--to remove all lies. A Life
Full of Holes was said truthfully at once from the
beginning. Therefore, we know it can be done. But
I am, like most of you, a middle-class person of
articulate origins. Like you I was considered ver-
bal and talented and then improved upon by interested persons. These are some of the lies that
have to be removed.

1. The lie of injustice to characters.
2. The lie of writing to an editor's taste,
or a teacher's.
3. The lie of writing to your best friend's
taste.
4. The lie of the approximate word.

5.   The lie of unnecessary adjectives.
6.   The lie of the brilliant sentence you love the most.

13.   Don't go through life without reading the autobiographies of
Emma Goldman
        Prince Kropotkin
                Malcolm X

14.   Two peculiar and successful assignments. Invent a person--that is, name the characteristics and we will write about him or her.   Last year it was a forty-year-old divorced policeman with two children.
        An assignment called the List Assignment. Because inside the natural form of day beginning and ending, supper with the family, an evening at the Draft Board, there are the facts of noise, con-flict, echo.   In other years, the most imaginative, inventive work has happened in these factual accounts.
                    For me too.
15.   The stories of Isaac Babel and the con-versation with him reported by Konstantin Paustovsky in *Years of Hope*.   Also, Paustovsky's *The Story of a Life,* a collection of stories incorrectly called autobiography.
        Read the Poem "The Circus Animals' Desertion" by William Butler Yeats.

        Students are missing from these notes.   They do most of the talking in class.   They read their own work aloud in their own voices and discuss and disagree with one another.   I do interrupt, inter-ject any one of the preceding remarks or one of a dozen others, simply bossing my way into the dis-cussion from time to time because after all, it's my shop.   To enlarge on these, I would need to keep a journal of conversations and events.   This would

be against my literary principles and pedagogical
habits--all of which are subject to change.

Therefore: I can only describe the fifteen
points I've made by telling you that they are
really notes for beginners, or for people like myself, who must begin again and again in order to
get anywhere at all.

(From *Writers as Teachers/Teachers as Writers*, ed.
Jonathan Baumbach, Holt, 1970).

Richard Perry

(From *The Summer Is Ended, and We Are Not Saved*,
a novel in progress)

I don't mean to sound as if Marcus was a monster.
I loved my brother. When I was a child, I ido-
lized him. But he was so obviously my father's
favorite that I felt excluded and I grew to resent
him. The resentment peaked in the days before we
left for Mississippi. I hadn't planned to go
south. Changing the world was not important to
me; it is not important now. I was going to
college in the fall to study photography. I was
not happy in that house. My father and I had had
a fight; he wouldn't forgive me. He was upset
because of Marcus; he had vowed that Marcus would
not go to Mississippi. He'd begun to drink heavi-
ly, alternated between brooding and rage.

•

    In my father's relationship to Marcus Garvey,
my brother said, could be found the key to my
father's craziness about Marcus going to Mississippi. A very long time ago my father had served as
Garvey's driver and bodyguard. That was in the
summer of his sixteenth year; he'd been big for
his age. A year and a half later, a brutal winter
found him married with a baby on the way. At the
insistence of my mother, who complained of a lack
of money, he'd quit and gone to work in a meat-
packing plant. And though he'd kept his membership
in Garvey's organization, he wasn't where he should
have been, at the side of the man who'd been his
leader and spiritual father. Because of his absence, the federal agents had come and taken Garvey without a fight. A man who would not protect
that which was important to him was less than a
man, and my father had never forgiven himself.

Through Garvey, my brother said, my father had had an opportunity to change the condition of black people in America, and he had, by acceding to his wife's demands, allowed circumstances to prevent him from doing so. And now his children had inherited this condition, and the unarmed efforts of his oldest son to change it could conceivably cost that son's life. It was not, Marcus said, a legacy to ease the heart of an aging man, and it was this guilt that had driven him to drunkeness and rage.

I don't know about all of that. I know that my father insists to this day that Garvey was framed. I know that my father was betrayed by a person or persons he would not name. I know that on the day he went to prison for plotting to break Garvey out of jail, a baby girl was born to my mother. That was February, 1925. The baby lived for three days and died in the midst of vomit and a strangulated cry, the result, my mother said, of milk gone bad from worrying.

Two years later, a month after Garvey was deported, my father, carrying a brown paper bag, dressed in the suit one size too small for him, walked through the prison gates into a morning so drunk with sunlight he thought his heart would burst. His wife was waiting, sat on a bench in an arboretum festive with birds and blossoms. When she saw him, she stood as if startled, as if her waiting was some penitent ritual outside the fortress walls, and her husband's appearance this morning miraculous answer to habitual prayer.

Testing the solidity of earth beneath his feet, the ease with which the body carved passage through unrestricted space, my father went to her. He spoke in the tone that men reserve for solemn occasions and took her home to resume their lives together. Neither he nor my mother mentioned why until much later, but there were no more children until Marcus, and by then my father had been home from prison sixteen years.

I remember the morning Marcus told me he
was leaving for Mississippi. We were on our way
to the hotel where we worked as busboys. He was
talking about the beauty and nobility of passive
resistance as if he had invented it. The day
was glistening. The rhythms of his voice suggested
song.

"Listen," he said. "You're my brother,
right?"

"Yes."

"And you love me?"

"Of course."

"I'm going to tell you something and you got
to promise not to tell."

I knew what he was going to say. I didn't
want to hear it. "Marcus," I began, but the sun
was full in his face, making his eyes glitter, his
skin turn bronze. I asked when he was leaving.

"Sometime in the next two weeks."

I didn't know what to say. I knew how he was.
I did not doubt his appreciation of the theory of
nonviolence; I doubted his ability to apply it.
He had never backed down from a fight. Even on
those occasions when he'd been badly beaten,
there'd been something inside him that would not
admit defeat, a persistence that had driven much
larger foes to attempts at conciliation, and finally
to desperation and tears. I had heard enough about
Mississippi to know that it denied the existence of
men like Marcus; I knew he would go out of his
way to confirm it. And he would be destroyed. I
needed to say this to him, but I felt that to say
it was to make it certain. So I just stood there,
speechless and stupid, and then I asked if he were
scared.

"Scared?" He grinned. "I'm scared to death."

His answer moved me. It was one of the rare
times that I heard him admit to uncertainty or
fear. Things were mixing in my gut, my own fear,
great love, and when he looked at me his face
seemed thin and brave and very young. I watched

his face until I couldn't stand it.

"But what about Daddy?"

He shrugged and stopped smiling. "He does what he got to do. I do what *I* got to do."

Like countless others of my generation, he had joined the movement. Like many of them, he became a casualty. But his wounds did not consist simply of disillusionment, nor even of the bruises and broken bones of beatings. This would not have been enough for Marcus, who, in addition to his pride, or because of it, possessed an almost theatrical sense of the gesture, the statement made not with words but with action. Getting his brains blown out by a shotgun at point-blank range was a dramatic statement. But he was my brother, and it left him dead.

I did not know any of this that morning. Though I was afraid for him, I had not learned enough about the world to imagine his ending in such graphic terms. I don't think Marcus had learned enough, either. He only knew that he was young, strong, and committed, and that the world was out there, ready to be conquered.

FICTION: RECREATING THE EXPERIENCE

"We had the experience, but missed the meaning," T.S. Eliot writes in "The Dry Salvages." For me, writing fiction is an attempt to recreate my experience and to discover its meaning. I do not mean by experience simply what I've done or what has happened to me. Experience includes books I've read, conversations overhead, dreams, fantasies, and especially feelings. This definition, which expands rather than limits possibilities, can be helpful to student writers, many of whom claim they

have nothing to write about. But it can also lead
to protests that "this or that experience is too
personal for print." To this I reply that everything is personal, and that the protest is nothing
more than acknowledgement that fiction is revela-
tory.

This acknowledgement should not provide an
obstacle to writing fiction. First, the result
of recreating experience is not necessarily autobiography. Second, if the experience *is* uncom-
fortably autobiographical, there are fictional
conventions (point of view, characterization, etc.),
all of which are functions of technique and imagination, behind which the writer can hide. None
need know that one secretly wishes to kill her
brother, or, as a child, hanged the family cat.
Create characters who despise felines or siblings.
The reader won't suspect the author.

This reassurance, however, skirts the issue.
How much of our experience is so uniquely awful as
to warrant keeping it hidden? Sometimes I ask
students to think of three "personal secrets,"
and to write down the least threatening of the
three. Then I read them out loud, anonymously.
Students are struck by the fact that many of the
"secrets" are similar. Several are met with mild
derision: "How could anyone be embarrassed about
that?" Occasionally, there are one or two "secrets" whose nature captures everyone's attention
because they are unique and, therefore, interesting.
I read them James Baldwin's statement: "It is
precisely the point at which the writer feels that
he is revealing too much of himself that he becomes interesting."

Of course this discussion leaves the students
still facing a number of questions. What experience will be recreated? Who will be the narrator?
How will the tone, the mood, the rhythms of the
narrative voice be arrived at? Seldom can these
questions be answered without trial and error.

Begin, I suggest, with freewriting. Discover
what's interesting to you. Resolve to tell the
truth. Get that first draft completed without
worrying about how things hold together. At some
point, maybe the third draft or the seventh, you'll
recognize that it's working. If not, don't des-
pair; try something else.

The preceding excerpt from a novel in progress
is one example of how I answered the above questions
for myself. It tells of the impact of the summer
of 1964 on the lives of several Civil Rights workers
who were active in Mississippi. Eight years later,
the narrator, Jason Strong, is recreating the history that contributed to his brother's decision to
go to Mississippi, which resulted in his brother's
politicization and recent death.

I've never been to Mississippi. Neither
has any of my brothers. But I've been interested
in the subject for many years. I've talked to
people who were in Mississippi in 1964; I've
read about the experience and have imagined being
there. I am familiar with rage, fear, racism,
death, and love, and the consequences of these
in my relationships, particularly those between
my father and me, and between me and my brothers
and sisters. I wanted to recreate these emotional
environments so that I could understand a little
more of who I am and, in the process, tell a
story.

The other questions: voice, tone, mood,
rhythm, became matters of characterization as soon
as I discovered that the narrator would be Jason.
Jason has always been detached, observant, con-
trolled. Photography, his profession, allows him
to exploit and justify his personality. Grieving,
he is incapable of irony; here his tone is sober,
objective. His rhythms are measured, broken now
and then by a lyricism that is a component of his
artist's vision. The mood of the piece reflects
his mourning; it is elegaic, commemorative, and,
at times, confused.

The rest is mystery.

Armand Schwerner

THE WAY UP IS THE WAY DOWN
*with some material from Robert Kelly and Ted
Enslin*

so often
as if earth had a trachea
full of dust
I envision my sons Adam and Ari falling through
  the street

'as if earth had a trachea'
that was your phrase but
I envision my sons Adam and Ari falling through
the street;
that wasn't what you had in mind?

that was your phrase but
I was drawn to an image of falling;
that wasn't what you had in mind
father?

I was drawn to an image of falling--
the way up is the way down--
father
did you used to have such pictures?

the way up is the way down
so often
did you used to have such pictures
full of dust

THE BROTHERHOOD AND THE SENSATIONS OF HAPPINESS
*with materials from Milarepa and from second-
and third-order American and Italian computer-
generated Shakespearean monkeys*

to dea now nat to be will and them be does
    doesorns
when I think of this my heart is filled with
    grief
I open the words *True, House, Hill, Porcelain*
or soon will fade or vanish.

when I think of this my heart is filled with
    grief
the gluepot of mind orders the rose
or soon will fade and vanish
as toise mosen to all yours you hom to to

the gluepot of mind orders the rose
self-control will still be hard. Though now you
    feel
as toise mosen to all your you hom to to
I can't touch you

self-control will still be hard. Though now you
    feel
like my teacher, crystal skull increasingly
    transparent,
I can't touch you
eselices hall it bled speal you...

like my teacher, crystal skull increasingly
    transparent,
the stoned rhetor in me divagates
eselices hall it bled speal you...
unattached to any home

the stoned rhetor in me divagates:
I envision my sons Adam and Ari falling through
    the street
unattached to any home
entre trintior e e desultto isenore si itolanon

I envision my sons Adam and Ari falling through
   the street
how I love the sensations of happiness
entre trintior e e desultto isenore si itolanon
quanta

how I love the sensations of happiness
I feel they deliver
quanta
of light

I feel they deliver
to dea now nat to be will and then he does
   doesorns
of light
I open the words *True, House, Hill, Porcelain*

The two poems above, pantoums--an old Malaysian
form--are composed in the most rigorous of the
paradigms presented in poetry "handbooks." Note
how the lines are repeated in a set pattern. The
last stanza must contain no new material. These
two poems came (in) directly out of work done with
4th- 5th-and 6th-grade children in Poets-in-the-
Schools programs. Obviously I've played with
the form in my versions, introduced further variables, but the pantoum is a natural for working
with children: it provides both structure and
"accident."

•

I'd expected a little period of warm-up, or
necessary repetition, but the children caught on
quickly. I think some aspects of their *Pac-Man*
and *Ms. Pac-Man* eye-hand-mind development pre-
dispose many children to skilled and accustomed
acceptance of symmetry, mathematical pleasures,

abstract paradigms--all in the context of Game--
that is, a profoundly poetic matrix.

That line 2 becomes line 1 of the following
stanza (line 4 becoming line 3) pleases many
children all the more when they are given the
liberty of disposing of any rhetorical level
for their "original" contribution in lines 2
and 4 of any new stanza: colloquial, technical,
hieratic language, whatever.... The pleasures
of the relatively random.... Not quite that
"anything can follow anything" but almost. And
such openness helps penetrate the rust of habitual image-thought-feeling attachments.

The nearly magical "found" final stanza under-
lines for the children the extent of the poten-
tially "meaningful." Since none of the lines of
the final stanza is written by the poet particularly for that stanza, since in fact they must all
come from, be born out of, the preceding or
subsequent (first) stanza, a kind of hunter's game
ensues. Which "last" of the possible "last"
stanzas will actually work, and what does it mean
to *work*, to "end"? So the whole question of
absolutistic unitary "meaning" imposes itself.
In a certain sense, almost anything works somewhat. But, observably, some "endings" appear
more relevant than others. Thus, some pantoums
arrive at their end in three stanzas, whereas
others require, say, 7, 9, 14.

The pantoum form encourages punctuation to
acquire a dramatic character. In the "brotherhood" for instance, line 4, which precedes a
period and also ends the stanza, takes on a different character, periodless, in stanza two as
it leads in to the "meaningless" monkey morphemes
of line 8. Quite often a "last" stanza becomes
possible through the use of strategically situ-
ated punctuation or italics.

My use of the form partakes of a greater degree
of complexity than the usual class poem, but the
added variables, found materials from areas of
interest to me, the cannibalizing of one poem by
another, great variations in line lengths, the
use of quotation marks for distancing, recessing
lines from the linear course of expected flow--
all such processes become increasingly available
to students, *on whatever level*, as they open to
the limitless adventure of making/finding poems.

Sometimes we work as a group. Here's a 5th-
grade pantoum:

hang in there baby
since green cars tend to hit red cars
get a bike or a camel and change your life
pray for snow

since green cars tend to hit red cars
how can I get through the day?
pray for snow
maybe stay in bed and dream

how can I get through the day?
too many bad news bulletins
maybe stay in bed and dream
blue cars, happy days, steak and mushrooms

how many bad news bulletins
hang in there baby
blue cars, happy days, steak and mushrooms
get a bike or a camel and change your life

Meredith Sue Willis

The Harley Davidson Motorcycle Company didn't buy
Garland's essay, but they did send him a hood or-
nament in the shape of an early, classic motorcycle. He brought the letter from the company
to school, and we had a big discussion about how
it differed from the business letter paradigm in
our textbook. Gail was particularly offended by
the absence of paragraph indentation. "Mrs.
Morgan!" she said to our teacher, my mother.
"Look at this! They skip a space instead of in-
denting. That's just plain wrong."

"How can it be wrong?" said Garland. "It's
a business letter, and they're a business."

"What does a motorcycle company know about
grammar?"

"What does a grammar book know about business?"
And the boys in the back clapped and cheered for
Garland. They seemed to have grown taller and
more colorful during the argument. In the end
Mother ruled that both forms would be hereafter
acceptable, and the boys shook one another's
hands as if they'd won some kind of victory.

To tell the truth, I thought they had. That
night Mother told Daddy all about how she had the
boys writing letters to gun manufacturers and
car companies. "You should have seen them,
Lloyd," she said. "Garland Odell and that big
Nathan Critch discussing whether to sign a business letter 'Sincerely' or 'Yours truly.'"

"That must have been real edifying," said
Daddy, who didn't very much like her having success with boys he'd written off as troublemakers.

"What gets me," I said, "is that the girls
study hard all the time, but the minute some boy
does his homework you teachers run out and kill

the fatted calf." Daddy chuckled, so I went on.
"Nobody gives the girls credit for doing their
homework night after night, year in and year
out--"

"I believe," said Mother, "that the credit for
doing homework is to earn a satisfactory grade.
I believe that that is generally considered credit enough for most people."

"It isn't just grades I'm talking about. It's
the way you all get excited about the boys and
try harder for them. It's just like the prodi-
gal son; that parable always sounded to me like
a recommendation to sow wild oats."

"Hear, hear," said Daddy. "Get that girl
a soapbox."

By this time I knew he was making fun of me, but
I plunged ahead. "It's always like that. The
geometry teacher would draw baseball diamonds on
the board and have us find the angle of the base-
lines at home plate. Anything to attract the boys'
attention."

"Equal time for girls!" called Daddy. "Assign
them to write recipes."

"I just don't like special treatment for boys,
that's all," I said. I had a vision of Daddy
as the kind of kid who snickered with his friends
over women and others who took things seriously.
He would have put a mouse in Mother's desk, I
thought, or chased me with a worm. The kind of
boy who, in the end, would never listen to what
you really had to say.

(From *Higher Ground*, Charles Scribner's Sons,
1981)

SOME THOUGHTS ON DIALOGUE WRITING

The longer I teach, the more I see the intercon-
nections between my fiction writing, my teaching,
and my reading. Thus, while I don't use my own
work as a model for student writing, I do use
work by adults that I admire and emulate. I
find myself teaching the same techniques and
themes that concern me in my own writing.

Dialogue, for example, is often central to
my work. A typical novel chapter of mine begins
with a reflective, relatively dense and meta-
phoric passage mixed with necessary narrative
material, then moves through various actions to
culminate in some face-to-face confrontation in
which people speak directly to one another. Dialogue, then, is often the dramatic heart of my
fiction, as well as its most naturalistic element.

I find dialogue to be an excellent point for
many students to begin writing because of this
potential for drama and this approximation of
everyday language. Children don't have to be
instructed about what conversation is. They can
improvise one on the spot, remember one, write one.
It is a natural connection between the spoken
word and the written word. The assignment can be
as simple as to dictate to yourself an actual conversation you have overheard or participated in.
The immediate success of this approach is especially attractive for students who are behind in
their academic skills. With younger children you
can do something further with the dialogue--act
it out, make a play, make a comic book. Perhaps
best, however, is that dialogue can realistically
and directly express some of the great themes of
human interaction: love, family conflict, hate,
reconciliation.

One of my absolute all-time-favorite-most-
successful lessons uses such a passage of dia-

logue-centered fiction from Tillie Olsen's
Yonnonidio: From the Thirties (Delacorte, 1974).
I organize the lesson in the traditional way--
reading the passage aloud, letting some students
take a turn reading aloud, then leading a short
discussion about it.

> No one greeted him at the gate -- the
> dark walls of the kitchen enclosed him like a
> smothering grave. Anna did not raise her head.
> In the other room the baby kept squalling
> and squalling and Ben was piping an out-of-
> tune song to quiet her. There was a sour
> smell of wet diapers and burned pots in the
> air.
> "Dinner ready?" he asked heavily.
> "No, not yet."
> Silence. Not a word from either.
> "Say, can't you stop that damn brat's
> squallin? A guy wants a little rest once in
> a while."
> No answer.
> "Aw, this kitchen stinks. I'm going out
> on the porch. And shut that brat up, she's
> drivin me nuts, you hear?" You hear, he
> reiterated to himself, stumbling down the
> steps, you hear, you hear. Driving me nuts.

Something about this piece sets off strong
reactions in many diverse people. It is beauti-
fully written, and it uses many fictional techniques: it creates an atmosphere with powerful
sense impressions; it contrasts the speaking
styles of the man and the woman; it has an internal monologue that intensifies the drama and
uses repetition to good effect. There is even
a neat grammar lesson available in the variant
spellings of "squalling" and "driving." One
writing assignment is to write a conflict of

your own, real or imaginary, or to continue this
passage or write what came before it. Many
people, even very young children, assume that the
man has just lost his job. I am always impressed
by this awareness of what happens to a family
when the economic machine catches the breadwinner
in its gears. Some students like to give a
happy ending, and others will send the man walking
out on his family permanently. Others have the
woman get up off her behind to come out and give
as good as she got.

Leashawn Peaks, a seventh grader at an East
New York intermediate school, continued the story
this way:

> You hear, he reiterated to himself,
> stomping down the steps, you hear, you hear.
> Driving me nuts. I can't take it here no
> more. First I lose my job, then I have to
> come home with this house smelling the way it
> do. Then on top of all that I have to hear
> this baby cry all the time. Don't you think
> a person gets tired of this all the time?
>
> So what do you think I do? Do you think
> I sit on my butt all day long and relax and
> have a maid wait on me? *No!* I don't, I be
> in here working my *hardest*. I try to keep
> this house running.
>
> Well, it don't look like you doing a
> darn thing in this house. I'm leaving. (As he
> walks to the door.)
>
> Where are you going?
>
> Out.
>
> She said, Wait, don't leave. You know
> you need me and I need you. We could work
> something out between us. I think we can
> patch things up. Let's give it a try.
>
> OK, he tells her. You know I love you
> and I don't know how I could stay mad at you,
> because I need you.

        All of a sudden the phone starts to ring.
Hello, is Mr. Johnson there?
        Yes he is.
        Well, can I speak to him? Hello, this
is Mr. Jones your boss. Hey man you got your
old job back.
        Thanks man, thanks alot. Hey Helen!
Guess what? I got my job back. I knew that
things would work out for us.

    Leashawn began by copying the final words of
the monologue--changing "stumbling" to a word she
felt more comfortable with, "stomping" -- then
continued the conversation between the man and
woman outside, as if the wife had followed him out.
She immediately gets at the heart of the matter as
she sees it. The husband and wife feel put upon,
as if each were carrying the burden of the family
completely alone. They have a reconciliation: an
adolescent's hope that after all it is possible to
work things out--and find employment as well.
    The selection from my own writing that precedes
this essay, an excerpt from my second novel, includes part of a teaching episode along with a
family conflict. It was not, of course, written
in the company of 30 or so other people in a
twenty-minute writing session after hearing the
selection from *Yonnonidio*. It does, however, show
how dialogue is woven through my fiction. Several
conflicts are going on simultaneously here, continuing
things that happened earlier in the book, preparing
for things to come later. There is a subtle competition between the parents and a more open tension
between the narrator and her mother, and the narrator and her father. There is also a conflict in
school between the "good" girls and the bored boys.
No one screams or gets murdered, but the mode is
of human voices speaking, expressing conflict and
connection. This is, after all, why we write.

Jeff Wright

FROM NOW ON

    There is no time to explain.
    I realized there was nothing left
in the L pocket of my accordian file.
    I realized I could say nothing right,
the right way.
    I realize I haven't changed
my whole life
the warm pool John's uncle took us to
    in downtown London.
Even our school group went once to swim
    at a private gymnasium & health spa.
Wickery girls I remember thru the mist
    rising with a chill off the tile
their long hair cadenzaed under plastic caps.

I still go for the same old things, old
    hotels, history, fairy tales &
working mothers, teachers, big brothers
    & dolls.

I told Linda Boswell she was a doll
    We called her Bod 's well or Bodswell
    8th grade swimming party hot dog tanned
cheeky fur machines out of control we
    played with razors & gushed
around young women like Linda who came
    up late with a boy in his V-8

I still go for the same old stuff
    Rock & Roll, vision, deception, focus
Deception is vision, vision is focus

W H I R L A W A Y
Short-Term Workshops with the Elderly

When I first started teaching a few years ago,
with the Teachers & Writers Artists & Elders
program, it was in long-term workshops. With
recent funding cuts, though, I've been limited to
workshops that consist of no more than three
meetings. To match the kind of intimate searching
and self-direction that evolve in a prolonged encounter, I have to be very focused, condensed,
spontaneous, and demanding.

In so few sessions my main concern is to begin
a process that will lead to an individual's continued writing. For several reasons, the journal
is the perfect genre for this. The journal (or
notebook) is an open form that allows for all kinds
of writing: personal prose narratives, poetry,
formal verse, dreams, domestic observations, reminiscences, and so on. Also, a long-term project
such as the journal helps bind the group together
by giving direction in the absence of a teacher,
and sympathetic group members validate an individual's writing by reading and listening to each
other's work and by suggesting ways the work might
be improved.

Keeping in mind the people I am working with, I
choose an author as a model who will appeal to
them. This often leads me to consider work I
would not ordinarily be drawn to, yet which may
eventually inform my own writing.

In order to accelerate the gradual development
process that accompanies journal keeping, I sort
out recurrent themes or elements and propose them
to the students. I ask them to make a list of
these points of entry into the text and use whatever parts they feel comfortable with.

Such a list might include dates, dreams,
quotes/old sayings, names, mini-portraits, colors,
firsts, reminders, predictions, and an addressee/

personal you. At this point I give some examples
and ask the group to use the list in writing a
brief journal entry. I use the list to create
a work myself, and as we read our works aloud
I find the group provides part of the anticipated
reception necessary to create character in writing.

This is not an iron-clad list. To make the
writing fun, convincing, and genuine I have to
invent new elements for each assignment, to keep
it exciting. This pressure forces me to understand the connections that justify the disjunct
elements of such works.

I admit I have an inordinate curiosity about
the people I work with. To satisfy this curiosity
I encourage writing that is expansive in its
brevity and depends on colossal leaps from one-
liner to one-liner or stanza to stanza, empha-
sizing the silence between thoughts, but providing
a few precise details which suggest a much
fuller version of themselves. If you had found
some gloves on a ship, what color were they and
what was the ship's name? Such details give me
a picture postcard version of the author's time
and place. I ask all the students to title their
works at the top (like a poem) and also to date
them at the top (like a journal), which hints at
considerations of merging all kinds of literary
forms.

I think these journal-like works can be as
evocative as a poem or short story and achieve a
personal voice without the embellishments of formal verse and the restrictions of linear prose
narrative.

In asking for this kind of writing I have had
to examine what holds a work together, what uni-
fying devices mesh the past and the present and
promote a clear, honest voice.

As a final, consolidating step, I steer the
students clear of generic titles, such as

Rambling Thoughts, and suggest they pretend they
are naming a boat, a racehorse, or a movie.
W H I R L A W A Y is still my favorite of all
these titles.

In a way I'm asking the writers I work with for
what I need as a writer myself. I'm saying share
your experience with me. Tell me this, this, and
this. And although I'm programming them to give
me data from their lives, from the books they've
read that contain others' lives, and from the
archetypes in their dreams, it's not all that
predictable, really, because the exchange is too
spontaneous to be preprogrammed.

TIT FOR TAT

You've shown me the back of your hand.
    You who are so bad.
You've shown me glass ships at Red Hook.
    I who have never sailed.
I showed you how to play chess.
We listened to Chopin's nocturnes.
We listened to the boys in the backyard playing
rock.
    We listened to each other while
    the white jasmine slyly eavesdropped.

            --Bensonhurst (N.Y.) Group

121

Bill Zavatsky

BASEBALL

We were only farm team
not "good enough" to
make big Little League
with its classic uniforms
deep lettered hats.
But our coach said
we were just as good
maybe better
so we played
the Little League champs
in our stenciled shirts
and soft purple caps
when the season was over.

What happened that afternoon
I can't remember--
whether we won or tied.
But in my mind
I lean back
to a pop-up hanging
in sunny sky
stopped
nailed to the blue
losing itself in a cloud
over second base
where I stood waiting.

Ray Michaud who knew
my up-and-down career
as a local player
my moments of graceful genius
my unpredictable ineptness
screamed arrows at me
from the dugout
where he waited to bat:
"He's gonna drop it! He
don't know how to catch,
You watch it drop!"

The ball kept climbing
higher, a black dot
no rules of gravity, no
brakes, a period searching
for a sentence, and the sentence read:
"You're no good, Bill
you won't catch this one now
you know you never will."

I watched myself looking up
and felt my body rust, falling
in pieces to the ground
a baby trying to stand up
an ant in the shadow of a house

I wasn't there
had never been born
would stand there forever
a statue squinting upward
pointed out laughed at
for a thousand years
teammates dead, forgotten
bones of anyone who played baseball
forgotten
baseball forgotten, played no more
played by robots on electric fields
who never missed
or cried in their own sweat

I'm thirty-four years old.
The game was over twenty years ago.
All I remember of that afternoon
when the ball came down

is that
I caught it.

WHAT THEY TAUGHT ME

I always balked when students wanted to see the
poems I wrote. I fended them off with promises
I never kept. Bringing them my own work seemed
like an ego-trip. The classroom wasn't the place
for career advancement. Then one day it dawned
on me that I *couldn't* show them my poetry. What
would a fifth-grader make out of lines like
these?

> Lexicons provoke a kind of madness
>   in me,
> Of the quality of too white, too
>   clean sheets.
> How many words, like brides, must
>   I lay my head against
> Until I can talk again, until I
>   can reach up and seize
> A radius of day larger than mind,
>   unlike the clown
> Shot and bandaged on the floor of
>   my father's face?

This work was tough going, grist for the
adult intelligence. Some of its meaning escaped
even me, though I believed in every word. Out of
desperation I sat myself down and wrote several
poems that I *could* read to kids. I tried to make
them funny, colorful, mysterious, full of details
and metaphors. The poems proved successful enough,
but after a while I stopped using them. Most
poems written by adults for children strike me as
phoney, and finally so did mine. I don't like the
spirit of enforced cheeriness that pervades them,
like a disinfectant used to mop up life's stronger
smells. If I couldn't bring my "difficult" poems
to class, I wasn't going to turn myself into a
spiritual janitor.

The difficulty in my work that my teaching
had revealed came as a blow. I had labored long
and hard on my poems, assuming that the images
discovered by my diligence would effectively
communicate my thoughts and feelings. The blank
expressions on audience faces when I read my
"serious" work away from the classroom (including
"The Presentation of Self in Everyday Life"
quoted above) compounded my uneasiness. I knew
the arguments by which I could shake off this un-
pleasantness. One of them contends that the audience is always years behind the poet (an appeal
to snobbism). Another shifts the burden to the
reader. A lot of poetry *is* difficult, says this
defense, and it isn't the poet's duty to explain.
A third asserts that poetry has always had a small
audience, so not to worry if the hall is empty
or your book doesn't sell. All of these arguments
have merit, and all of them pass the buck. It was
never the fault of the writer if his work went un-
read or unappreciated. The poet discharged his
responsibility by producing the poem. Case closed.

But the puzzled classroom faces that I coaxed
through contemporary poems fused in my mind with
the frozen stares of the poetry reading crowds.
Mine weren't the only poems receiving blank looks.
The work of plenty of my contemporaries and even
well-known poets usually found itself greeted by
a puzzled silence often interpreted (by the poet)
as reverential awe. Puzzlement can be an extremely
productive condition. It is not, however, the
only reaction that a writer might hope to induce.
The only measurable reaction at readings was
laughter, but laughter leaves many things un-
touched. As I began to examine poetry from the
perspective of a non-poet, much of it struck me as
introverted to the point of narcissism or re-
served for cliques. Few poets wrote about a rec-
ognizable world. There was a good deal of '60s

"canyons of my mind" surrealism and even more
word-play. Where were the faces, places, jobs,
families, love-relationships, delights, and
struggles that made up our lives? What had
happened to story in poetry? Most of us poets
behaved like amnesiacs wandering through the
corridors of the thesaurus.

I had spent a lot of time hiding in and behind words rather than using them as conscious
instruments. For me, language had become a screen
to filter out direct examination of my life. I
had become adept at scooping up the dream and fantasy images bubbling from my unconscious, but not
very skilled at writing about what I saw when I
was wide awake. Perhaps my preoccupation with
the oddball and the hallucinatory had something to
do with the *zeitgeist*. America *was* pretty looney
in the late '60s and early '70s, with its
Vietnam War, drug culture, rock music, and endless
waves of every kind of revolution. Then too, my
religious background had tilted my gaze upward
away from this "vale of tears." Likewise, the
school of poetry in which I took my flight train-
ing had as its insignia the flaming metaphor. By
the time these things became clear to me I knew
that I had to pull my head out of the dream. I
had to wake up.

At the beginning of my work with children, I
eagerly involved them in the crazy kind of poetry
I loved. Nevertheless, I always had one eye on
the kids who didn't take to it--and there were
many of them. It disturbed me, but then and
there I simply lacked the means to give them anything else. After twelve years of teaching, I've
concluded that very few writers have a real gift
for metaphor. Does that mean they can't become
poets? Yes, if metaphor is the yardstick by which
poetic accomplishment is measured. And I believe
that in our schools it is. American education

and the various poetry-in-the-schools programs
have wedded creativity to fantasy, whose chief
vehicle is the metaphor. The problem with metaphors is that they are mental constructs; though
formed from the things of this world, they lead
us away from it. To paraphrase Ezra Pound's
famous little poem, faces that are also petals
on a wet, black bough exist not in the Paris Me-
tro but in the mind.

My work with children taught me that they are
capable of seeing clearly and writing about
what they see. As I began to immerse myself in
this kind of "experiential" writing, I also encouraged my students to write about what had
happened to them and what they remembered rather
than only about their fantasies. I insisted
that "imagination" included fantasy *and* memory.
I haven't abandoned the "wild" metaphors I've
always loved. I've sought to balance them with
outer perceptions, and I try to equip my students to do the same. The poem called "Baseball," included here, dates from the mid-seven-
ties and shows me learning how to be ambidex-
trous, how to mediate between inner and outer
worlds.

I feel a little sorry for poets who don't
teach writing, or who rarely read their work in
public. In facing an audience I have had to
reach inside myself or into the work of others
to find poems that will call forth more than a
giggle or stony silence. My students have forced
me to extend myself by demanding authenticity
of feeling and experience. They have brought me
closer to reality simply by being there. No one
can go consistently into the classroom and remain
unchanged. And in responding to the faces before
me, the old bond of poet as community voice finds
itself somewhat restored. These are some of
the things the children have taught me.

Alan Ziegler

1981

Each year I make more money
and my purchasing power decreases.
In this I am not alone.
Still, I have managed to acquire recently:
a watch, camera, answering machine,
coffee maker, shirts and sweaters.
I wonder how I got along before.
Sex is less important,
Or rather, it's more important
so I do it less.
Strangers call me "Mr."--nothing new
but I no longer pause before answering.
My family has suffered no losses.
My sister has added two;
I, none.
I am in love but we are not together,
which is, I suppose,
better than the opposite.
I have accepted as fact that
I will never catch up with work
but most things get done eventually;
also, that summer is not as long
as the rest of the year,
so expectations must be adjusted accordingly.
I worry less about colds and the flu,
more about cancer and heart attacks.
I am 34
and so is everyone else
in my high school and college classes,
though they can't all say
as I can
that they weigh the same now as then.
I don't get the desire as often
to grab someone by the shoulders
and say, "Listen to me, look at me,
don't you *understand?*"
But when I do,

it's sadder when they don't.
At 16, Wordsworth wrote about
"dear delicious pain."
At more than twice that age
I no longer think pain is delicious,
though some is palatable.
I no longer open my pores to everything
simply because it's *there*,
but when I do,
I drink long and deep.

FOLLOWING MY OWN ADVICE

On an old Pete Seeger album, Pete tells of hearing
his younger brother play a banjo tune "so pretty
that he put me to shame." His brother explained
to Pete that "it's nothing more than double
thumbing while you're frailing," and Pete re-
plied, "I talked about that but I never really
knew how to do it." So, he went on, "I sat
down and followed some of the advice I put in
my own banjo book and I practiced." Sometimes
my students write things that inspire me to
follow my own advice. Other times, just having
the opportunity to talk about areas in writing
that are new and/or elusive to me enables me to
sift, mull, and sometimes get a hold on something tangible that will inform my writing.

Such a case was the importance of notebooks
as a repository for spontaneous thoughts and
sights and sounds of the day, along with notes
on possible writing projects--an ongoing internal
monologue.

I had talked about that but I never really
knew how to do it. I started giving my students
notebooks that they could use as they saw fit,
and many of them "put me to shame," notably
Isabel Feliz, a sixth grader who filled two notebooks with stories, poems, plays, and diary entries. One of Isabel's entries was a response

to my suggestion of writing occasionally to take
stock of your life, an inventory of the things
that are around you and inside you:

"I've often wondered *who* I am and where do
I belong....I mean who am I truly inside and
where do I belong truly inside?....It's not as
if I'm a shy and lonely girl trying to find her-
self or as if I'm a rich person trying to be
popular....I *have* a best friend, although we
have grown apart in the last few months....Maybe
sometimes I feel strange being alive, being
able to talk, move, hear and see....
"When a friend asks you, for example,
'Do you like that hat?' you ask, 'Do *you?*'
We ask them if they like it because we're
afraid of saying yes when our friend might
say no. Our friend might say 'You have bad
taste!'"

The students' prolific use of their notebooks
gave me a "contact high"--in the hallway I'd see
the books sticking out of back pockets, to be
pulled out as if by electrical impulse to record
a sudden thought, and I'd watch students choosing
to do first drafts in their notebooks--which,
after they were broken in, seemed more inviting
than a single sheet of blank paper.
I emphasized that the notebook is a place for
students to do *their* writing, not to be judged
or evaluated by anyone, including me, unless
they requested it. It took me awhile, but now
I utilize a notebook more than ever before.
My 1981 poem grew out of a notebook entry which
was an attempt to do my "inventory" assignment.
My teaching has served my fiction writing
even more than my poetry. Though the possibilities for poetry are limitless, any given poem
of mine tends to concentrate on one or two elements, such as description, internal monologue,

or metaphor. In fiction, many ingredients go
into each brew: characterization, setting,
presentation and working through of conflict,
dialogue, etc.

As I began to write more fiction I realized
that writing a short story can be overwhelming
and a novel megawhelming, so I started to teach
its separate components, giving assignments that,
though they wouldn't result in fully realized
stories, would allow students to concentrate on
specific areas. Meanwhile, I began to read fiction more sharply, to discern how writers make
characters reveal themselves; what writers tell
us about places so that we get a feel for that
place without bogging down in superfluous detail;
how they pace stories, speeding up and slowing
down the narrative. As I discuss these issues
in class, I am clarifying them for myself as
well as for my students.

●

I have always found it extremely difficult to
discuss the links between my writing and my
teaching. Sometimes it seems that this is because they are so separate; other times because
they are so intertwined. My concerns as a
teacher are dictated far more by the needs of
my students than by my needs as a writer. But
the public act of teaching and the private act
of writing rarely clash with each other, and
mesh often enough to make the slash between
writer/teacher a meeting point rather than a
barrier.

Contributors

NEIL BALDWIN has worked with Poets-in-the-Schools, Poets & Writers, and Teachers & Writers Collaborative. He is the author of two volumes of poetry; a descriptive catalogue of William Carlos Williams' manuscripts; *The Poetry Writing Handbook* (Scholastic, 1981); and a forthcoming biography of Williams for young readers (Atheneum, 1983).

BARBARA BARACKS' writing has appeared in *The Village Voice, Artforum, MS., Art Express, The Soho News,* and other publications and anthologies. A 1977 CAPS Fellow, and author of *No Sleep,* she has edited and published a literary/arts magazine titled *Big Deal,* co-edited *Sage Writings,* and is currently a member of the *Heresies* editorial collective putting together *Acting Up!: Women in Theater and Performance.* She has worked in the T&W program since 1979.

JONATHAN BAUMBACH is the author of seven books of fiction, including most recently, *My Father More or Less* and *The Return of Service.* His stories have been anthologized widely, including both major collections of the best stories of the year. He writes movie reviews for *Partisan Review* and his fiction has been influenced by the dreamlike quality of film. He directs the MFA Program in Creative Writing at Brooklyn College.

JUDITH BINDER has worked in the T&W program for the past three years. She spent several years in San Francisco as a theatre artist and writer. She has collaborated on scripts with poet/playwright Nina Serrano, historian Paul Richards, and filmmaker Irving Saraf. Her plays have been produced in the U.S., Canada, and Latin America.

CAROLE BOVOSO is a journalist and poet. A frequent contributor to the *Village Voice*, she has written for many national magazines, such as *Ms., New Dawn, Oui, Viva,* and *American Film*. She is the founder and editor of *Letters*, and she produces "Letters" radio show on WBAI in New York. For PBS's American Playhouse series she is currently writing a screenplay based on her great-grandmother's 1868 diary.

NANCY BUNGE teaches writing at Michigan State University and is currently working on a series of interviews with writers who teach. Her articles have appeared in *The San Francisco Review of Books, The American Poetry Review,* and others.

ANNE CHERNER is the author of *The Surveyor's Hand,* a book of poems, and has taught for T&W for five years.

JACK COLLOM works in the T&W program. Born in 1931 in Chicago, he has lived for many years in Colorado, now resides in New York. He is the father of four children and is an ex-factory-worker. He has led many poetry workshops in Colorado, Nebraska, and New York. For 11 years he edited the little magazine, *the*. In 1980 he received a Poetry Fellowship from the National Endowment for the Arts Literature Program. His most recent book is *The Fox* (United Artists Books).

BARBARA DANISH'S work with T&W resulted in her book on teaching writing, *Writing As a Second Language* (T&W). Her poems have appeared in *The Mississippi Review, Hanging Loose,* and *Aleph,* and the Feminist Press published *The Dragon and the Doctor,* a children's book. She also teaches at the College of Staten Island.

RICHARD ELMAN is the author of ten novels, five books of journalism, three of poems, and a collection of stories, all under his own name, and numerous pseudonymous works. He has taught in the T&W program and at the university level. He is presently book critic for National Public Radio's "All Things Considered."

HARRY GREENBERG has worked for T&W and the New York State Poets-in-the-Schools Program for the last five years. He is co-editor of the literary magazine *Some* and the Release Press book series. His poems have appeared in *Poetry Now* as well as many other magazines.

WENDY JONES, a newcomer to T&W, is living in re-write land this year. She is rewriting a short story to send to *Atlantic Monthly,* rewriting a novella for the *Quarterly West* novella competition, and rewriting a novel for publication.

KENNETH KOCH's work with T&W resulted in *Wishes, Lies, and Dreams* and *Rose, Where Did You Get That Red?* He is also the author of a book of plays, *A Change of Hearts*; a novel, *The Red Robins*; and 10 books of poetry, the most recent of which is *Days & Nights*. He is professor of English at Columbia University.

PHILLIP LOPATE'S work with T&W is chronicled in his *Being with Children* (Doubleday), *Journal of a Living Experiment* (T&W), and his many articles for *T&W Magazine*. His books of fiction and poetry include *Confessions of Summer* (Doubleday), *Bachelorhood* (Little, Brown), *The Eyes Don't Always Want to Stay Open* (SUN), and *The Daily Round* (SUN). He teaches at the University of Houston.

DICK LOURIE worked in the T&W program in the late '60s and early '70s. For 16 years he has been associated with Hanging Loose Press, which published his most recent collection of poems, *Anima*. A founding member of the N.Y. PITS program, he is currently working in the Massachusetts PITS program.

CLARENCE MAJOR is the author of 12 books of prose and poetry. He is the recipient of fellowships from the National Endowment for the Arts, the New York Cultural Foundation, and the Fulbright Commission. He worked in the T&W program in the late '60s; currently he teaches at the University of Colorado.

MIGUEL A. ORTIZ taught in the T&W program and was for many years Director of Publications at T&W. He is associated with Hanging Loose Press.

ABIODUN OYEWOLE teaches for T&W and the NYC public schools. An original member of The Last Poets, he writes plays *(Comments)*, stories, poems, and songs. He performs with his jazz group, Griot.

RON PADGETT has been associated with the T&W program since 1969. With Bill Zavatsky he edited *The Whole Word Catalogue* 2 (McGraw-Hill/ T&W, 1977). Among his other books are *Great Balls of Fire* (Holt, 1969), *Toujours l'amour* (SUN, 1976), *Triangles in the Afternoon* (SUN, 1979), and *Tulsa Kid* (Z, 1979). He is Director of Publications at T&W.

GRACE PALEY was one of the founders of T&W. Widely published, her two most recent collections of stories are *The Little Disturbances of Man*, (New American Library) and *Enormous Changes at*

the Last Minute (Farrar, Straus & Giroux). She
teaches at Sarah Lawrence College.

RICHARD PERRY, a member of T&W for eleven years,
also teaches literature and writing at Pratt
Institute. He is the author of *Changes* (1974)
and *Sparkle* (1976). His most recent novel,
Montgomery's Children, is scheduled by Harcourt
Brace Jovanovich for fall 1983 publication.

ARMAND SCHWERNER is the author of 14 books of
poetry, the most recent of which is *Sounds of
the River Naranjana* (Station Hill Press), which
includes the two pantoums in his article. He
worked in the early T&W program and with the
Academy of American Poets 1967 prototype of
PITS. Recipient of grants from the National
Endowment for the Arts, he currently works in
the New York State PITS program.

NANCY LARSON SHAPIRO is the Director of
Teachers & Writers Collaborative, where she
has worked since 1976. She has taught writing
and English and been an editor for small
presses and at Encyclopaedia Britannica.

MEREDITH SUE WILLIS has taught writing workshops
for students from first grade through college and
senior citizens. Her novels, *A Space Apart* and
Higher Ground, are both published by Charles
Scribner's Sons. She has worked for T&W since
1971.

JEFF WRIGHT is the author of *Employment of the
Apes* (poems) and editor of *Compass* magazine and
Hard Press postcards. For the past three years
he has conducted writing workshops for the elderly, including T&W's Artists & Elders Project.

BILL ZAVATSKY has worked in the T&W program for many years. He has also taught writing and literature to university students and the elderly. *Theories of Rain,* his collection of poems, appeared in 1975. With Ron Padgett he edited *The Whole Word Catalogue 2.* He is currently completing a book about the film *Rebel Without a Cause.*

ALAN ZIEGLER has taught for T&W since 1974; he also teaches at Columbia University. His most recent books are *The Writing Workshop* (T&W) and *So Much To Do* (Release Press).

THE THINK/INK SERIES

The Point: Where Teaching & Writing Intersect
edited by Nancy Larson Shapiro & Ron Padgett.
T/I 1/2 (double number).

Reading Your Students: Their Writing & Their Selves
by Anne Martin. T/I 3.

Poetry Comics in the Classroom
by Dave Morice. T/I 4.

Think/Ink Books are published by Teachers &
Writers Collaborative, 84 Fifth Avenue, New
York, N.Y. 10011 (212/691-6590).